A Horse is a Horse, of Course:
1st International Symposium for Equine Welfare and Wellness:

Compendium Part II

© 2017 Ilka Parent/Minds-n-Motion



## Disclaimer

The information provided in this publication is for general informational purposes only. All contributing authors remain responsible for their contributions and have signed contributor agreements stating that all sources and publications have been rightfully cited and quoted. All activities involving horses have inherent risks, including danger to body and limb. Any individuals who wish to participate in equine-assisted psychotherapy should do so only under appropriate psychotherapeutic care. Any practitioners who wish to participate in equine assisted psychotherapy should do so only after receiving appropriate training in either the mental health profession or equine biology. The author does not make any representations or warranties as to the information in this publication and expressly disclaims any and all liability arising out of participation in or utilization of any techniques, experiences or activities involving horses.

CONTENT

EDITOR'S NOTE .................................................................................... *XI*

INTRODUCTION  ................................................................ *XIII*

**A Horse is a Horse, of Course**

*Ilka Parent*


CHAPTER 17 ..............................................................................*27*

**Human-Horse Interactions and Relationships – Relating, Bonding, and Attaching**
An Introduction

*Ilka Parent*


CHAPTER 18 .............................................................................*37*

**Understanding and Employment of Horses Using the HEAL Model of EFPL**
An Introduction

*Leigh Shambo*

1.    How is the Horse Viewed in HEAL? .................................................*38*
2.    Theoretical Rationale for HEAL EFPL as Part of Therapy .........................*44*
3.    EFPL Activities and Strategic Set-Up ...........................................*45*
4.    Progression of Therapy in Stages ...............................................*46*
5.    Glimpses into a Course of Treatment with EFPL ..................................*47*
6.    Theoretical Foundations/Resources for HEAL Model Practice .....................*50*
7.    Assessing the Well-Being of Therapy Horses ....................................*50*

CHAPTER 19 ...................................................................................................*55*

**The Human-Equine Relational Development (HERD) Approach**
Incorporating Equines in the Psychotherapeutic Process

*Veronica Lac*


CHAPTER 20 ...................................................................................................*67*

**A Sentience-Based Approach to Equine-Facilitated Interactions**
From Theory to Practice: Building Professional Partnerships with Horses

*Angela Dunning*

1. More on How I View Horses: ...................................................*68*
2. My Theoretical Approach ........................................................*69*
3. Why I Work with Horses and People ......................................*71*
4. The Horse's Role ......................................................................*72*
5. Differing Interpretations of the Horse's Feedback ..................*73*
6. Case Examples .........................................................................*74*
7. How I Ensure the Horses' Welfare and Well-Being ................*77*
8. Equine Consent & Choice .......................................................*77*
9. Freedom of Movement ............................................................*79*

CHAPTER 21 .........................................................................................................83

**The Journey to Healing ... Through the Eyes of the Horse**
*Marlene du Plessis*

1.   The Brain, the Body and Behavior .................................................84
2.   Logotherapy ..................................................................................90
3.   Equine Assisted Therapeutic Facilitation: The Theory ..................94
4.   Equine Assisted Therapeutic Facilitation – as Experiential Therapy ............96
5.   Why Do We Use Horses? ...............................................................97
6.   How does Equine Assisted Therapeutic Facilitation Work? .........100
7.   The Best of Two Worlds ...............................................................101
8.   The Process in the Facilitation Space ...........................................108
9.   Conclusion ...................................................................................113

CHAPTER 22 .......................................................................................................117

**Horses as Sentient Beings in Psychodynamic Equine Assisted Trauma Therapy (pEATT)**
*Ilka Parent*

CHAPTER 23 .......................................................................................................125

**Somatic Experiencing® and Attachment Principles**
Increasing Safety and Welfare in Equine-Assisted Interventions and Horsemanship Approaches

*Sarah Schlote*

1.   The Activation Cycle Map ............................................................127
2.   Fostering Safety Via Titration ......................................................133
3.   Attachment as a Somatic Experience ...........................................138

CHAPTER 24 .................................................................................... *147*

**Joy of Creative Writing with Horses**
Cases of Therapeutic Encounters

*Pirjo Suvilehto*

1.    Introduction ................................................................ *148*
2.    Theory of Human-Animal Studies ........................... *149*
3.    Theory of Bibliotherapy ........................................... *151*
4.    Equine-Human Well-Being and Togetherness ........... *153*
5.    Equine Moments ...................................................... *154*

CHAPTER 25 .................................................................................... *159*

**A Horse is a Horse, of Course – Heart Connection**
*Eva Balzer*

CHAPTER 26 .................................................................................... *171*

**Pepper – Project Trauma Support**
*Dr. Manuela Joannou*

CHAPTER 27 ..............................................................................................*185*

**The Role of the Horse**
The Therapeutic Philosophy of Horse Sense of the Carolinas, Inc.

*Shannon Knapp*

1.   Concept of What Promotes Change .........................................................*186*
2.   Process-Focused vs. Goal-Focused .........................................................*186*
3.   Learner-Centered, Experiential Approach ...............................................*187*
4.   Power Dynamics & Gurus ......................................................................*187*
5.   Team Approach ......................................................................................*188*
6.   Value of and Purpose of the Horse ........................................................*189*
7.   The Role of the Horse in Equine-Assisted Psychotherapy .......................*189*
8.   The Instinct to Flee ...............................................................................*190*
9.   Opposition Reflex ..................................................................................*191*
10.  Clean Listening: A Different Agenda ......................................................*191*
11.  More than a Mirror ...............................................................................*192*
12.  Facilitator and Client Engagement: 3D vs 2D .......................................*193*
13.  Use & Tool Debate ................................................................................*194*
14.  Horses & What's in it for Them? ...........................................................*195*
15.  Summary ...............................................................................................*196*

CHAPTER 28 .......................................................................................*197*

**Natural Lifemanship's Trauma-Focused Equine Assisted Psychotherapy (TF-EAP)**
The Connected Relationship is the Vehicle for Change for Human and for Horse

*Laura McFarland, PhD, Bettina Shultz-Jobe, MA, LPC, and Tim Jobe, BS*

1.   A Brief History of the Model ........................................................*199*
2.   Trauma-Informed Care and Natural Lifemanship ......................*201*
3.   Basic Brain Development of Humans and Horses ......................*202*
4.   Core Principles of Neurodevelopment ........................................*204*
5.   The Horse Brain and the Human Brain ......................................*209*
6.   The Principle of Choice: Cooperation is Predicated on Choice. ...*215*
7.   How a Horse May Experience the NL Principles on the Ground .....*219*
8.   How the Principles Extend to Mounted Work ............................*220*
9.   Summary ........................................................................................*223*

CONCLUSION ...................................................................................*227*

# EDITOR'S NOTE

Throughout these articles, many written by non-native English speakers, I have tried to keep the authors' style and tone while conforming with colloquial English. Some articles are more formal and were edited to maintain their scientific and scholarly nature. Others were more personal and anecdotal. These were edited appropriately in order to maintain the more conversational tone. Another goal of my editing was to ensure that each article would be understandable to the layman. For the sake of uniformity, all spelling except for quotations, reflects standard American English spelling.

*-Kenneth Burland*

INTRODUCTION

# A Horse is a Horse, of Course

Ilka Parent

*My passion for horses started, from what I am told, when I was not even two years old. There were riding stables close to where I grew up, and my parents would take me there for "pony rides". It must have been the highlight of my life back then, as I would ask every day when we would go "riding". At four, I started vaulting – doing acrobatics on horseback. I loved everything about horses – their smell, cleaning them and their stables, and, of course, being with and around them. So, it is understandable that I wanted to combine a later profession with horses as well. However, I was encouraged to pursue a profession with more outlook and sustainability, and to keep horses as my hobby instead. But the dream, the desire was there, and, whenever I could, I would find horses who needed to be ridden and taken care of, and would volunteer my time in exchange for any moments I could spend with them.*

I did not get my first horse until I was 27 years old. Horses were far more affordable in the United States than in Germany, which finally made it possible to pursue the dream of owning one. I met Monty, an Arabian gelding, by now 27 years old, and he taught me more about humans and myself than anybody else. Monty was abused, and it took serious time and effort to get him rehabilitated. He was flighty, easily spooked, considered dangerous and untrainable. In the first 8 months of knowing him, I didn't ride him – we would just spend time together, explore El Paso and its surrounding desert, and get to know each other. 18 years later we maintain a relationship that is built on trust, mutual respect, and understanding that evolved during those years. No one considers him dangerous anymore. Instead, he has helped and carried a multitude of people and helped them work through their own traumas. He is, to this day, my "soul horse", and, even though I no longer live in the same country as he does, he still recognizes me every time I go visit.

My introduction to Equine Assisted Psychotherapy (EAP) started in 2005. The dream of combining my "real" work (Psychotherapy) with horses never ceased, and I quickly started implementing EAP with several of my horses in my private practice. My experience with Monty shaped my outlook on their well-being. Working primarily with trauma and knowing about its effects on mental health providers enabled me to keep a trauma informed lens not only for the people with whom I was and am working, but also kept me keenly aware of the effects this work might have on the horses. I got to know them very differently and was more than once surprised by what I saw transpiring in sessions. I also, unfortunately, particularly during my work as trainer, witnessed negative effects of EAP on horses, with them colicking after sessions or developing so-called "vices" due to the work. All of the above led to my questioning certain practices and wanting to advocate more and more on behalf of the horses – which made me realize that there are many, many unknowns about them. How do they contribute? What do they really perceive? What are really the effects of EAP and equine facilitated practices on the horses? Questions and more questions started to arise.

Parallel to developing those questions, a trend materialized in the world: more and more, the psychotherapeutic, personal growth, and coaching market was flooded with a variety of modalities that advertise the incorporation of animals, given the overwhelming evidence that they can assist in improving a person's well-being. But each approach and/or organization claims its own view about the role of equines and what they bring to the equation as presumably herd and flight animals that respond differently to their environment than humans. Many claim being the best and only one putting forth standards and principles, with the horses' well-being in the forefront. Always being on the curious side, an idea started to form for me. Instead of me comparing methods and models and approaches, I wanted representatives of these different approaches and trainings to present their own perspectives, with the horses' well-being in the forefront. In this way individuals – readers – could form their own opinions and find their own answers based on the information provided; because all of the certifying organizations have one thing in common: The horse. And a horse is a horse, of course – right?

Based on my own experience, I found that saying to be fitting for the exploration of equine wellness and well-being in more depth, especially because my own perception of horses has changed so much over the years in working with them. What do we really know about how they think, what they feel, how they perceive and interact with each other and with us? What impact do horse-human interactions and programs have on them? What do they need? Are we acting ethically with their best interests in mind? Personally, I work from a psychodynamic framework, and in pEATT (psychodynamic Equine Assisted Traumatherapy), I established guidelines and standards as to how one is to work with them (instead of utilizing them) and how they are contributing. I consider the horses an integral part of my work, and even though I practice in office without them, I regard them highly and favor equine assisted Traumatherapy to in-office therapy. Putting forth ethical guidelines on how to work with them was of particular interest to me, as in Germany, horses (and other animals) are still considered (judicially) "objects" that can be treated in many ways which do not necessarily protect their rights as sentient beings. But I also wanted to know more about other perceptions and practices, particularly those teaching the techniques and skills relating to the work in our field. I decided to put the first of a series of symposiums together to explore these questions further. I sent out a call to the international community of equine interaction professionals offering equine-assisted or facilitated therapy, learning, coaching, or other similar interventions. The call was answered by numerous individuals worldwide, hailing from Germany, the UK, France, the Netherlands, Sweden, the USA, and Canada, with training in many of the most well-known approaches, including EQUUSOMA Equine-Facilitated Trauma Therapy, Natural Lifemanship, Eponaquest Approach, HEAL, Learning Animals, Integrative Equine-Facilitated Wellness, TTouch, and LEAP, among others. I wanted to see if there was evidence for supporting the notion of recognizing equines as sentient beings deserving of having a choice and a voice; beyond strictly seeing them as tools that are secondary to the process. My intent was to have an array of speakers presenting a range of contrasting, complementary, and contradictory views, providing a snapshot of the diversity in the equine assisted/facilitated field. The first international Symposium on Equine Wellness and Well-being was held in Wartenberg-Rohrbach, Germany, from July 11-13, 2017. It was a complete success with international attendance.

My long-term mission is to improve the safety, care, and well-being of horses, donkeys, and mules in equine interaction programs through science, compassionate inquiry, and interdisciplinary collaboration. I was assisted by Katarina Felicia Lundgren and Sarah Schlote with their time and contributions in planning for the event. Apart from providing a resource for professionals and others interested in the field of Equine Assisted/ Facilitated work, my continued goal is to raise funds for the Minds in Motion Education and Research Centre (MiMer)[1], an organization with a trust set up to help fund research on equines, human-equine interactions, and equine-assisted interventions. All proceeds of this and future compendiums will go entirely towards supporting this research – all contributions and work to make this possible have been donated and given for free. This and future symposiums are also intended to create a platform for speakers in our field to publish a compendium of papers about their topics, to make the information more easily available to all those willing and wanting to learn more about the four-legged beings who so greatly contribute to the work we do.

The following book is the result of my call and includes the articles of the 2017 symposium presentations and articles of those in our field who wanted to support my vision. Due to the large volume of submitted articles and information, I decided to publish two volumes: In *Volume One*, equines are explored in depth, taking into consideration biological, cognitive, psychophysiological and behavioral traits and dynamics, drawing from the fields of cognitive science, trauma neuroscience and ethology. In *Volume Two*, the welfare and well-being of horses in specific equine assisted/facilitated programs are being looked at more closely. Both volumes contain symposium presentations as well as

---

1   MiMer, although in cooperation with Ilka Parent and Minds-n-Motion, is an independent research center. Ilka Parent is not affiliated with the center other than through a contractual cooperation agreement pertaining to all funds obtained through current and future symposiums as well as compendiums going into future research to help promote the equine assisted/facilitated field and equine welfare and well-being in it.

articles submitted by authors who could not attend the symposium. Articles and speakers were chosen based on how much they represented varying viewpoints to ensure a non-biased, informative compendium.

Volume One starts out with *Rhys Evans'* article "Horse work in the 21st Century". He points out that just as the nature of work has changed for humans, horse work has also changed. With this change in the nature of work, it is necessary to alter our approach to dealing with horses and the new demands and requirements necessary for the horse's well-being. This will require re-educating horse owners as well as veterinarians who will need to alter their approach to providing the necessary care and maintenance of horses in their new roles.

In the article "The Horse as a Biological Being", *Katarina Felicia Lundgren* examines the evolutionary development of the horse both before and after contact with humans. The author looks at the ways in which horses in captivity differ from horses in the wild and how these differences lead to varying behaviors. Especially important is the concept of horses having sufficient space in their living environment.

Looking further into "Equine Cognition and Human Interaction", *Katarina Felicia Lundgren* points out that a key factor in providing for the well-being of horses is the understanding of how horses think and why they react in certain ways. Domestication has altered the conditions under which a horse lives and it is necessary to find ways in which the formation of relationships between humans and horses can be beneficial to both species. Clearly a horse working through its own issues will not be well-suited as a therapy horse. Understanding what the horses are telling us will provide a safe environment for both the horse, the client, and all involved in the therapy.

In her third article, "Sharing Minds", *Katarina Felicia Lundgren* explores the question as to why equine therapy is so effective and what the relationship between horse and human is that promotes meaningful interactions. The author looks at the theory of intersubjectivity which helps explain how horses and humans can mutually benefit from equine assisted therapy.

Starting from the proclamation *"A stallion is a horse as well"*, in her article *Epona Domengès* discusses "The Therapeutic Power of Stallions", how she developed Alternative Equitation and Equestrian Art Therapy, and why she is committed to having only stallions involved in the therapy process. She further details what she considers the best ecological and spatial environment for horses, and especially for stallions.

In the article "The Inside of a Man-made Herd", *Vanessa and Wanda Lee-Jones* explain how they moved from the traditional rows of single horse stalls to the creation of a more normal herd environment for their horses. The authors delineate the responsibilities of the owners to take care of their charges but also go on to discuss the best, most natural environment for horses, donkeys, and mules.

*Nicola Mahon* analyzes the use of the Tellington TTouch method of massage to promote a better sense of well-being for the horse and to establish a positive relationship between horse and human in her article "Integrating TTouch". The TTouch method provides a physical conversation and encourages the development of a sense of empowerment for the horse.

*Nina Ekholm Fry* sees us at a crossroads with our horses. The focal point in her article "Love Is Not Enough" is a quotation from a client who observed that "this is my paradise, but I don't think it's theirs." In the therapy process the horse needs always to be considered and understood in order to provide the safest environment for all concerned. This understanding is crucial in EAP. This understanding needs to be based on accurate information and assessments and there is a great deal which we still do not understand.

One of the methods we use to explain the world around us is via metaphor. But, as *Dana Adriana Ignat* points out in her article "Mirror, Mirror", meaning is often lost in the manipulation of words. One such example is considering a horse to be a mirror for humans. Such an approach can lead to misunderstanding and misinterpretation of reality. What is really important here is silent, spontaneous body language through which the horse communicates and becomes a competent emotional communication partner.

In looking out for the welfare of therapy horses, it is necessary to have clear definitions of terms such as horse stress and horse burnout. In the article "Best Practices", *Cryshtal Avera* points out that these definitions are lacking as are any standardized procedures for establishing best practices. She provides a framework and starting point for the establishment of horse care standards within the industry.

In looking at therapy horses, *Amanda Ball* emphasizes the need for a holistic approach in her article "A Quadrant Approach", which also includes a spiritual aspect. Most writing about EAP deals with the physical, emotional, and the intellectual parts of the horse and the client while omitting the spiritual. She sees the ground where horse, client, and counselor meet as a sacred place that allows for self-discovery.

*Leanne Nieforth* and *Elizabeth A. Craig* discuss the significance of creating the best atmosphere for the horse's welfare in their article "Horse Welfare in EAP" through the development of a relationship built on trust and freedom. The horse must be given the opportunity to engage or not engage with a particular client. The equine specialist is vital in this process as a conduit through which the horse communicates.

Humans have always had a fascination with horses. As the horse has been replaced by machines, there may yet be a new and important role for the horse. The horse has several qualities which can assist the human to improve physically, emotionally, and spiritually. But can they be considered to be therapists? *Nathalie Durel* addresses this question in her article "Can We Consider Horses to Be Therapists?".

Starting from childhood, *Christine Fairweather* shares her life-long love of horses that has continued through her practice in equine assisted therapy. She explains the unique psychology of the horse and how this allows for the horse to be an integral part of the therapeutic process. She also explains the significance of the horse as a metaphor. Metaphor has long been used in therapy sessions as a means of establishing meaning. In her article "Incorporating Equine Assisted Therapy into an Integrative Model of Practice", the author explores how much more powerful the metaphor is when it is part of non-verbal communication with a horse. The horse is a teacher, healer, role model, and metaphor when engaged properly.

Though differing in particulars, all mammals share certain neurological and physical characteristics. In her article *Sarah Schlote* examines "Applying a Trauma Lens", especially the similarities between horses and humans and why it is necessary to apply the same perspective or lens toward the horse as it is toward the client. In the same way that we encourage humans to have a balanced life of play, work, and socializing, it is necessary to ensure that horses have the same opportunity for balance and just to be horses.

Volume One concludes with *Susanne Weis'* article. She expresses how she felt that traditional trainings methods were lacking something. She explains how changing the focus from demanding responses from horses to establishing a dialog with them creates the opportunity for true growth in both the human and the horses.

Volume Two focuses on the welfare and well-being of horses in specific equine assisted/facilitated programs. *Ilka Parent* discusses in her introductory article "Human-Horse Interactions and Relationships – Relating, Bonding, and Attaching: An Introduction" the necessity of staying aware of the needs of these horses. She argues that transference and countertransference, psychoanalytic concepts, can more readily occur between horses and humans than simply between humans. This is facilitated by the fact that horses are non-judgmental, accepting, and are more easily approached and touched. While the benefits of EAP for humans is becoming more obvious, it is necessary to take into consideration how this therapy impacts horses.

*Leigh Shambo* was one of the founders of HEAL (Human-Equine Alliances for Learning). In her article "Understanding and Employment of Horses Using the HEAL Model of EFPL", the author describes the model: This model promotes mindfulness and a constant awareness of the horse as it is involved in therapy sessions. In order to promote the optimal situation for the therapy horse, she presents six keys by which to assess the horse's well-being.

In her article, *Angela Dunning* explains "A Sentience Based Approach to EAP" her sentience based, consensual partnership method of horse therapy. The key is that all aspects of the horse need to be considered in order for the treatment to be mutually beneficial. Besides the normal physical care, it is important to understand the natural rhythms of the horse in terms of temperament, perceptions, and volitions.

In her article, "The Human-Equine Relational Development (HERD) Approach", *Veronica Lac* explains her HERD approach: a five-stage model designed to assist the client in becoming existentially aware of and acknowledging heretofore unacknowledged needs. The horse and the client are brought together on equal terms and the herd's ability to self-regulate is always respected. The key factor is that the horse and client form a completely willing partnership.

In her article "The journey to Healing .... Through the Eyes of the Horse", *Marlene du Plessis* begins with a look at how individuals are wired to deal with the external world and how this is impacted by trauma. When patterns of communications and relationships are disrupted through trauma or abuse, it is possible to rebuild positive interactions and replace older, destructive patterns. Equine therapy assists in helping the client to have an active and accountable role in trauma treatment.

*Ilka Parent* explains the theory behind psychodynamic Equine Assisted Trauma Therapy in her article "Horses as Sentient Beings in psychodynamic Equine Assisted Trauma Therapy (pEATT)". Her approach to trauma therapy considers each member of the team, both two- and four-legged, to have considerable rights and responsibilities. A team consists of a licensed psychotherapist, an equine specialist as connoisseur of horses' body language, at least one client and at least one horse. Working together, the entire team creates a safe environment for all of the participants.

When mammals experience trauma, there are many responses such as the freeze responses. Once the danger has passed, the animal re-sets and continues on. For humans, this process of re-setting can be quite different. In her article "How Somatic Experiencing and Attachment Principles can Increase Safety and Welfare", *Sarah Schlote* discusses the EQUUSOMA approach to trauma treatment through the incorporation of the horse into this process.

Art and horse activities are combined for *Pirjo Suvilehto*. In her article "Joy of Creative Writing with Horses" the author describes how creative expression combined with equine therapy sessions allows an individual the opportunity for self-expression with the horses to provide a sense of security and well-being during the creative process. In this bibliotherapy, the horses are there as friends who help in the process of a deeper self-understanding.

In her article "A Horse is a Horse", *Eva Balzer* discusses the Kiron method of trauma therapy which was developed in Portugal and is based on the myth of Centaur Chiron, the archetype of the wounded therapist. The Kiron method is based on re-creating, as closely as possible, the natural environment of the horse, and the horse is given complete freedom to participate in or to reject participation in the equine assisted intervention.

*Manuela Joannou* discusses her life-long love of horses and how horses can be effective in the treatment of PTSD in her article "Pepper – Project Trauma Support". She looks at the unique characteristics of horses and why they are such special creatures.

Horses are extremely valuable in EAP to *Shannon Knapp* because of their honest, non-judgmental feedback. In her article "The Role of the Horse", the author asserts that the true benefit of horses in equine assisted therapy is the integration of thoughts, feelings, and senses which they help to bring out. She also points out the need to recognize that not all horses are suited to equine therapy.

Volume Two concludes with *Laura McFarland, Bettina Shultz-Jobe*, and *Tim Jobe*, who emphasize in their article "Natural Lifemanship" that the horse is an authentic relationship partner and not a tool. Their article focuses on the role of the horse in the therapy process. Natural Lifemanship seeks to create a relationship between horse and client that is based on connection rather than survival instincts.

My heartfelt "Thank You" goes out to all those who contributed to make this volume possible. My heartfelt invitation goes out to all who will join us at the 2nd International Symposium "A Horse is a Horse, of course", either by presenting, speaking, submitting an article or joining us in person. Yet my dedication goes to the horses – those beings who, by simply being themselves – add tremendous value to so many people's lives and certainly have added to mine.

Obermohr, November 13, 2017

*Ilka Parent*

PART II

# Equine Science and Welfare

CHAPTER 17

# Human-Horse Interactions and Relationships – Relating, Bonding, and Attaching

## An Introduction

Ilka Parent

*What takes place when horses and humans meet and interact in a therapeutic setting? Studies confirm that during any psychotherapeutic process, the quality of the relationship between the psychotherapist and the client has proven to predict a positive outcome with much higher accuracy than any chosen treatment method. But what happens in the human when the primary relationship is transferred to the horses? This presentation will provide a review of current literature. It will also look at the human psychological and physiological effects during human-equine interactions, how humans interact with their environment, how relationships are formed, what they typically consist of and what is necessary for humans to be able to bond and attach. This presentation will leave room for the reader to explore further the ethical considerations necessary to ensure the equines wellbeing in human-equine interaction programs.*

Many equine interaction programs focus on the relationship between clients and horses. Before looking at the effects of such interactions, it makes sense to first look at what "relationship" means.

All beings and objects relate to one another in one way or another – relations are normal phenomena of any life's process. Any life process takes place in an environment since there is no natural vacuum in the world in which we live. Life itself is bound to an exchange with the environment that surrounds it. Objects and animals alike co-exist with their surroundings and are in relation with each other. Creatures adjust to their environment: they react to it and influence it. Just imagine a flower in a flower bed. Imagine a bee flying to a single flower, landing on it, taking in pollen, then flying off to the next one. Each is touched, and an abundance of reactions and interactions are taking place.

Therefore, to understand any relationship, one must consider individuals as part of their environment. Interpersonal relationships between two or more humans are even more complex: the relation between individuals changes the quality of the interaction, as each individual brings with them personal qualities and differences in perception, reaction and action.

Before I go further, let me just state that any theoretical concept automatically implies a reduction of the essentially unlimited complexity of human relationships, and thus demands its price. However, I would not be a psycho-analyst by calling if I did not bring in Sigmund Freud, the founder of psychoanalysis. Among many things, he examined what takes place during the human-human interaction and looked closely at what happens when a therapist and a patient meet and interact in a therapeutic setting. He was the first to establish a client's right to self-determine his or her own topics in the doctor-patient context and looked at the developing dynamic as well as what typical reactions the therapist may experience in response to the patient. He coined the terms transference and counter-transference: Transference happens when we transfer feelings and attitudes from a person or situation of the past onto a person or situation in the present.[1] This is not a conscious or thought out process. As human beings, we connect certain emotions and associations with important people from our past. Technically, transference is the experience of feelings and attitudes towards one person in the present which has its origin in the relationship one has had with another person from the past. The term counter-transference implies a form of transference in which the psychotherapist reacts to the patient. It is the psychotherapist's thoughts, feelings,

---

1   The Fundamentals of Equine Assisted Traumatherapy, Parent, 2016

prejudices, wishes and expectations towards the patient. Freud saw this process as linear as the psychotherapist was to remain outside the interaction and stay abstinent.

Many of Freud's theories and paradigms have been questioned and developed further, especially by his disciples. Noteworthy are Michael Balint and Donald W. Winnicott, both object psychologists, who expanded the concepts of transference and counter-transference as being interactional and circular, meaning the therapists themselves, whether abstinent or not, started to be seen as important and influential in the here and now relationship. John Bowlby, a child psychiatrist and psychoanalyst, looked further into what it takes to form relationships: he observed small children in their reaction to being separated from their primary caregivers and formulated his attachment theory on those observations. Peter Fonogy, a Hungarian born psychoanalyst, expanded on Bowlby's attachment theory and put forth a detailed theory on mentalization and on regulating affect based on one's primary relationship experience. Mentalization is defined as the ability to make and use mental representations of one's own and other people's emotional states. He defines bad and insufficient parenting as the caretaker's inability or unwillingness to identify and/or detect emotional processes in herself and others; to understand, reflect back and to articulate, giving the child the opportunity to identify successfully himself; to detect and to articulate his own emotional states. An individual's attachment style and one's ability to mentalize has great impact on a person's ability to form and sustain relationships.

All of the above concepts come into play in human interactions, but what happens in interspecies relationships? What effects take place in a human-horse interaction?

Case Vignette:

*He had stated that he hated horses. "Meat and lasagna, that is what they are good for." The 48 year old veteran was hesitant to go out and try Equine Assisted Traumatherapy, but as most other therapies had failed he was desperate to get some kind of relief from his recurrent nightmares, flashbacks, a life that had ended in unemployment, with ongoing medical problems. He could not remember the last time he had slept through a night, and had withdrawn*

*from most people. His wife had left him, he no longer had contact with his children —
he lived a very solitary life filled with anguish and agony. He reluctantly committed to try
out at least four sessions of equine assisted trauma therapy.*

*During the next four sessions, there was not much conversation. After initially observing a
herd of horses, the client was asked to go out and meet them, introduce himself to them and
get to know them. His contact with the horses was brief, with them consistently turning
away from him when he approached them, or walking towards him yet brushing by him
quickly once they got close to him. He was asked to build his current situation, and build his
future anticipated (and wished for) situation on the other end of a path, which he was to
line with foreseen obstacles and hindrances. Most of the man's movements were quick, with
a rigid and seemingly tense body. He remained focused on building things, and labeling
them, and when he spoke, he mostly did so in terms of the current troubles and adversities
in his life. The creation of the path, with obstacles, and the ensuing invitation to walk the
path with "one or more four-leggers of his choice" took up three sessions. Initially, the man
could not approach the horses; there was a lot of movement seen with horses running and the
man moving quickly behind them. This picture changed to the man attempting to bribe the
horses, who seemed interested in the grass being offered to them, but not in moving anywhere
near the obstacle path. In the fourth session, the man appeared to be very frustrated and close
to giving up. He sat down in the middle of the path, with his head resting on his knees. He
was approached by one horse, an elderly horse, who thus far had not had any contact with
him nor with the other horses. This horse stayed with the man, his head hanging close to the
ground. It took several minutes for the man to notice the horse. Once he did, he stood up and
moved closer to the horse, who remained in place. They both simply stood side by side for a
very long time, until they proceeded down the path to the area that represented the future,
without stopping once. The man came back for a fifth session. He simply stated: "That horse
stood by me when no-one else did. I felt calmer and more relaxed than I have felt in a long
time. I enjoyed his presence. He gave me hope again and courage to not give up — and when
he walked with me made me aware that I need to and can take more steps. I want to go on."*

Julius et al. (2014) offers a comprehensive look at the psychological and physiological effects of human-animal interactions with implications for the therapeutic practice. The following will be a summarized review of their writing. The authors reviewed 66 empirical studies to summarize current researched effects of animals in human-animal interactions. Not all studies were conducted with horses; instead, some were with companion animals, particularly dogs. However, the authors argue that these effects can be transferred to horses as well:

1. In human-animal interactions, positive health effects could be noted. Studies indicate potential positive effects on the general health of pet owners, particularly cardiovascular effects: Pet owners who had suffered from a heart attack showed a higher survival rate afterwards.

2. A so-called "social catalyst effect" could be observed: Studies showed that having an animal present in a therapeutic setting facilitated easier therapeutic access to clients

3. It could be shown that the presence of animals improved learning in children with and without learning disabilities

4. Higher empathy could be measured in children and adults who maintained a close relationship to their pet.

5. The presence of animals led to a significant (self-reported) reduction in fear and increased calmness and relaxation

6. In group settings, increased trust and trustworthiness within group participants as well as towards the facilitator/therapist were reported when animals were present

7. Human-animal interactions led to a significantly increased positive mood and overall reduction of depressive symptoms

8. Increased pain management was reported as well as

9. An overall reduction of aggressive behaviors

10. Several physiological effects could be measured: studies primarily focused on the activation and deactivation of the stress system (Hypothalamus-Hypophysis-Adrenal axis)

    a. Cardiovascular parameters such as heart beat, blood pressure and neuroendocrine variables such as cortisol (hormone), epinephrine and norepinephrine in saliva and blood (stress indicators) were lower during stressful situation when animals were present

11. Overall positive effects on the immune system were reported

12. Effects on the oxytocin system

    a. Oxytocin influences and helps regulate social behavior, fear, stress, pain, tranquility, well-being, memory and learning. It is a hormone that is released through intensive sensory stimulation, e.g. while giving birth, nursing, or through a special type of relationship: bonding and attachment. We will look at these concepts in a later section. The nerve fibers that transmit oxytocin also reach the amygdala, the so-called fear center responsible for flight-fight-freeze responses. Oxytocin can initiate a so-called "growth & relaxation"/"calm & connecting" reaction.

Humans exposed to stressful situations typically react with increased activity of the sympathetic nervous system if the situation is perceived as threatening. The endocrine axis gets activated and cortisol levels rise. In the presence of supportive humans, the cortisol levels do not rise as much and the situation is not perceived as threatening – presumably due to an increase in oxytocin levels in the brain. As has been described in this book and Part 1 of the *"A Horse is a Horse, of Course"* Compendium, the fundamental biological structures and functions that serve to regulate social relationships are identical in humans and animals. One can easily conclude that "true" relationships between humans and animals are possible and that oxytocin is released in those interactions.

As was mentioned, the hormone oxytocin helps regulate social behavior. Oxytocin is released through bonding and attachment. Both concepts focus on the exclusive, close relationship between two partners: bonding primarily refers to the basal physiological and psychological mechanisms and is enhanced through the release of oxytocin. When bonded individuals are separated, anxiety and disquiet are experienced and behaviors are activated to reestablish closeness. Attachment refers to a particular way in which one relates to other people. John Bowlby's attachment theory includes the cognitive and affective representations of prior relational experiences with a primary caretaker.

Bowlby identified several different attachment styles: these are formed at the very beginning of one's life, during the first two years. Once established, it is a style that stays with a person and plays out in everyday life in how one relates within intimate and close relationships with another person or being.

When a person is born, he is helpless and dependent. He needs to develop a relationship with at least one primary caregiver in order for his social and emotional development to occur, preferably normally. Without this attachment, he will suffer long-term serious *psychological* and *social* impairment. Attachment styles are therefore formed in response to the way in which parents or caregivers respond to their infants, particularly during times of distress. The patterns formed in the early years will go on to guide the child's feelings, thoughts and expectations throughout his life.

Bowlby identified different types of attachments:

- Secure attachments are formed when infants experience a consistent caregiver who is attuned to them, that is, who is sensitive and responsive in their *interactions* with them. During the second year of life, children begin to use the caregiver as a secure base from which to explore the world and become more independent.

- Avoidant attachment is formed when the primary caregivers are emotionally unavailable and, as a result, are insensitive to and unaware of the needs of their children. They show little or no response when a child is hurting or distressed. These parents discourage crying and encourage independence. Often their children quickly develop into "little adults" who take care of themselves. These children pull away from needing anything from anyone else and are self-contained.

- Ambivalent/Anxious attachment forms when the primary caregivers are inconsistently attuned to their children. At times their responses are appropriate and nurturing, but, at other times, they are intrusive and insensitive. Children with this kind of parenting are confused and insecure, not knowing what type of treatment to expect. They often feel suspicious and distrustful of their parent, but, at the same time, they act clingy and desperate.

- Disorganized attachment is formed when a parent or caregiver is abusive to a child, and the child experiences the physical and emotional cruelty and frightening behavior as life-threatening. This child is caught in a terrible dilemma: her survival instincts are telling her to flee to safety. But due to the child's own (physical and emotional) inability and dependence, "safety" is the very person who is terrifying her. The attachment figure is the source of the child's distress. In these situations, children typically disassociate from their *concept of self*. They detach from what is happening to them and what they are experiencing is blocked from their consciousness.

All of the above childhood attachment styles form adult attachment styles:

- People who have formed secure attachments in childhood develop secure attachment patterns in adulthood. They have a strong sense of themselves and they desire close associations with others. They basically have a positive view of themselves, their partners, and their relationships. Their lives are balanced: they are both secure in their independence and in their close relationships.

- Those who have had avoidant attachments in childhood most likely will develop dismissive attachment patterns as adults. These people tend to be loners; they regard relationships and emotions as being relatively unimportant. They are cerebral and suppress their feelings. Their typical response to conflict and stressful situations is to avoid them by distancing themselves.

- Children who have an ambivalent/anxious attachment often grow up to have preoccupied attachment patterns. As adults, they are self-critical and insecure. They seek approval and reassurance from others, yet this never relieves their self-doubt. In their relationships, deep-seated feelings that they are going to be rejected make them worried and not trusting. This drives them to act clingy and overly dependent on their partner.

- People who grew up with disorganized attachments often develop fearful-avoidant patterns of attachment. Since, as children, they detached from their feelings during times of trauma, as adults, they continue to be somewhat detached from themselves. They desire relationships and are comfortable in them until they develop an emotionally close relationship. At this point, the feelings that were repressed in childhood begin to resurface and, with no awareness of them being from the past, they are experienced in the present. The person is no longer in life today but rather, is suddenly re-living an old trauma.

Even though attachment styles affect people throughout their entire life, it is possible to develop a "secure attachment" at any age. One way to change an attachment style is to experience a secure relationship.

How do these concepts and behaviors play out in Human-Horse relationships?

One can easily argue that transference and counter-transference cycles are broken: as the primary relationship takes place with one or more horses, people can project their emotions onto the horses, yet remain aware that horses will not respond like humans. Negative mentalization concepts are not transferred: a horse is a horse, of course! Due to this knowledge, the reluctance to engage in a relationship, to bond and attach to the horses, is lower than it is with a human counterpart. Animals appear to be social catalysts. Additionally, studies confirm (2006) that the resistance against physical contact with animals is lower than between humans. As was shown, physical contact releases oxytocin and lowers the release of stress inducing cortisol, accounting for self-reported lowered stress and anxiety. It quickly becomes evident that there are a variety of positive effects for humans in their interactions with equines – making it all the more important to consider and weigh the ethical implications for the horses.

**About the Author**

Originally from Mainz, Germany, Ilka Parent spent close to 20 years living and working in the United States. She earned her Diploma in Clinical Psychology in 1997 in Germany, and finished her psychoanalytical training in El Paso, Texas (1998-2003).

Having been married to a military service member for over 20 years afforded her the opportunity to work in various military departments and in private practice, primarily with active duty service members and their families. Ilka completed training in Equine Assisted Psychotherapy in 2007, and is certified at the advanced level of EAGALA. Consequently, she founded her company Minds-n-Motion: a private clinical practice and name that represents her pursuit to assist people putting their minds in motion through equine participation. Over the past 11 years, Ilka has continued to expand vastly on the EAGALA model by incorporating current psychotherapeutic and trauma approaches. Her primary population are military service members and people suffering from severe childhood trauma and other (combat related) traumatic experiences. Ilka returned to Germany in 2011 and established psychoanalytically based Equine Assisted Psychotraumatherapy (pEATT). As Minds-n-Motion has grown, she is offering training programs in Europe, the U.S. and other countries. She is author of numerous books about her work and perspectives on psychodynamic Equine Assisted Traumatherapy. She is and remains an avid advocate on equine welfare in equine-assisted modalities as well as trauma-informed treatment.

## References


Ainsworth, M.S. & Bowlby, J. (1991). An ethological approach to personality development. *American Psychologist*, 46(4), 333-341.

Bateman, A. u. Fonagy, P. (2008). *Psychotherapie der Borderline-Persönlichkeitsstörung: Ein mentalisierungsgestütztes Behandlungskonzept*, Psychosozial-Verlag; Auflage: 1.

Bowlby, J. (1975). Attachment theory, separation anxiety, and mourning. In D.A. Hamburg & H. K. M. Brodie (Eds.), *American Handbook of Psychiatry*, Vol. 6, New Psychiatry Frontiers. New York: Basic Books.

Fonogy, P. et al. (2002). *Affect Regulation, Mentalization, and the Development of the Self.* Other Press, N.Y.

Julius et al. (2014). *Bindung zu Tieren. Psychologische und neurobiologische Grundlagen tiergest Interventionen.* Hogrefe Verlag; Auflage: 1

Olbrich, E. (2003). Kommunikation zwischen Mensch und Tier. In E. Olbrich, & C. Otterstedt, *Menschen brauchen Tiere. Grundlagen und Praxis der tiergest Pädagogik und Therapie.* p. 85f. Stuttgart.

Parent, I.B. (2016). *Fundamentals of Equine Assisted Trauma Therapy.* CreateSpace Independent Publishing Platform.

CHAPTER 18

# Understanding and Employment of Horses Using the HEAL Model of EFPL

## An Introduction

Leigh Shambo

*As the Founder and Director of HEAL, I welcome this opportunity to share our view of the horse in EFPL. The HEAL Model has roots in my life as a horse-woman — teaching riding, training horses, and managing herds. From the beginning, I wanted to help equestrians shed the "emotional baggage" that affected their horses. I returned to school, and became credentialed as a MH therapist. In 2000 Human-Equine Alliances for Learning (HEAL) was born. HEAL has evolved and gained recognition as a cohesive therapeutic model for EFPL, focused on treating complex PTSD in children and adults.*

Our view of horses and our relationship with them are consistent with our *Six Keys to Relationship'* approach, as described in *The Listening Heart* (Shambo, 2013).

The Six Keys are summarized in Table 1, Affective Domains in HEAL's Six Keys to Relationship. The table provides an overview of our cohesive framework for EFPL. The reader may refer to it as I share our view of the horse, activities, and implementation of methods, and our theoretical foundations. A case summary will present glimpses of one client's treatment to illustrate the role of the horse in the HEAL approach. We will end with a Six Key guide to the care and support of therapy horses.

I will continue with the term EFPL (for Equine-Facilitated Psychotherapy and Learning) to describe our field, recognizing that some identify their equine activities as "assisted" or "guided", etc. Our choice of EFPL reflects our view, but is not meant to exclude anybody. I will refer to us collectively as *practitioners* or *facilitators*, whether therapist, counselor, coach, or teacher. I will refer to participants in EFPL as *clients*, whether they are "P" or "L". My intent is to explain our approach as simply as possible; not to comment or to compare with other methods. While we as EFPL practitioners sometimes disagree, we have more in common than we have dividing us. We are all passionate, even opinionated, in our care for the horses. We all value the voice and well-being of the horses involved. We practice diligent care both in and out of session, but none of us are perfect. Thankfully, horses are forgiving. The Sufi poet Rumi might have channeled a horse when he wrote, *"Out beyond ideas of wrong doing and right doing, there is a field. I'll meet you there."* Let's proceed to explore our topic!

## 1.    How is the Horse Viewed in HEAL?

### Shared domains of social-affective experience

I once heard Dr. Jaak Panksepp, the celebrated neuroscientist who mapped the brain circuits that mediate emotions in mammals, say of people and animals, *"-We are all brothers and sisters under the skin"* (Panksepp, 2012, Keynote). I liked the idea of seeing animals as our relations. In HEAL, we see the horse as having a *person-hood*. It is much different, of course, than human personhood, but it goes beyond the definition of sentience. My dictionary defines sentient thus: *responsive to or conscious of sense impressions; aware; finely sensitive in perception or feeling* (Merriam-Webster's, 2004). That describes horses, and many other animals as well. However, it does not fully capture the highly social, family-band-oriented mammals that horses are. At HEAL we see and describe the horse through relational metaphors that point to a healthy, balanced and caring interdependency with humans. Like us, horses are highly social animals whose emotional balance and wellbeing depends on the quality of their attached relationships, including with the humans in their lives.

Table 1. **The affective domains in HEAL's Six Keys to Relationship**

| Affective Domain (KEY) | Blue Ribbon Neural Circuit; Associated behavior prime | Stage of therapy in EFPL; skills and activities in horse relationship |
|---|---|---|
| Body Awareness Mindfulness **Key One** | **FEAR** / sense of safety Primed for avoidance or approach; escape, freeze. | **Beginning stage** Self awareness, becoming acquainted; noticing resonance; mutual choosing. Approaching, safety, haltering and leading, reading body language, self-awareness, gauging energy levels in self and horse, setting boundaries, reading boundaries, asking horse to step back, |
| Boundaries **Key Two** | **RAGE** / respect Primed to fight if trapped; but safe boundaries prime sense of deep safety. | matching strides, turning horse both ways, use of space bubble, use of breath, modulation of energy, safe touch and therapeutic touch, grooming. Sitting astride, going with, being carried by horse. **Emphasis on physical/emotional attunement** |
| Triggers-Defenses – Incongruence Grief and loss **Key Three** | **PANIC**/social belonging Primed to call for help; frantic attempts to fit in; fear of rejection; appeasing; social anxiety. | **Middle stage of EFPL:** Figuring out dynamics of the relationship, responding to disruptions in connection. Advanced boundaries, leading, the art of not-doing/learning to wait, advanced horse listening, asking for horse's attention, using the driving aid to ask the horse forward, |
| Initiation – Assertiveness Structure & Leadership **Key Four** | **PLAY** (rough and tumble) Primes: play signals, interactive competitive games; serves purpose of family and social structure. | challenge activities, exercising the horse, independent riding, directing horse's feet from the ground, able to ask for gaits in RP, boundaries in action. Leading away from herd, leading w/ neck rope. Basic clicker training. **Emphasis on the "rub" & mutual regulation** |
| Imagination, New possibilities **Key Five** | **SEEKING** (high drive state) Primes: to explore, investigate sniffing and searching. | **Culmination stage of EFPL** Performance and play based on practiced ability to read each other; Horse dancing, synchronous play, imaginative journeying, advanced exercises at liberty, riding out, |
| Bonding/Attachment The Social Brain Sacrifice, forgiveness, nuturance. **Key Six** | **CARE** (maternal/paternal, pair bonding & social bonds). Primes: Protect, nurture, seek proximity, generosity toward other, forgiveness and sacrifice. | advanced clicker –new tasks, creativity combined with horse work, creating positive endings, commemorating and anchoring experiences (photos, art work, celebrations, self-created ceremony or commemoration. **Emphasis on emotional revision/competence** |

Famous trainers Delgado and Pignon, in their book *Gallop to Freedom*, assert that the relationship between man and horse has no exact parallel; but they go on to say, *"[...] a good parent-offspring relationship is in some ways the closest: the parent will learn from the child and the child find safe haven in the parent... respect is a natural consequence"* (Delgado and Pignon, 2009, p. 32). Their "equine liberty" performances show the ultimate in human-horse intimacy and artistry. The horse is allowed freedom within clear boundaries and gentle authority. The parent-child metaphor fits such close relationships, but may not fit well for our clients' horse relationships.

The word *colleague* fits nicely. Many EFPL practitioners employ their own horses as therapy animals, while other practitioners may work primarily with horses at a center. Personally, I do both, and while my own horses feel like family, the horses I do not live with feel more collegial. All of us probably realize that employing a family member as a colleague can challenge our ability to see that individual realistically. On the other hand, if a horse is not in our direct care the challenge might be to develop a closer understanding as colleagues.

These relational metaphors encourage practitioners and clients to see horses in EFPL as individuals with attachment needs like ours. We are all affected by our relational history, and have possibilities for new growth in current relationships. The EFPL environment, often including other animals as well, is like a multi-species community, with the horses as members. For clients, the community offers a safe yet varied container for experiences with animals which replicate some aspects of important human relationships. These simple but feeling-rich relationships can literally help clients re-wire the neural circuits of social-emotional functioning. In HEAL therapy the capacity for emotional regulation, a two-way process that happens naturally between client and horse, will be made more conscious, will be cultivated and enhanced, and ultimately transferred to human relationships.

The HEAL Model also integrates science from various fields to inform our view of horses. Panksepp discovered that the neural systems of *primary* emotional arousal – organized around the brainstem and limbic structures of the brain – are *essentially similar for all mammals including humans* (Panksepp, 1998, p. 60). While the brainstem governs instinctive action tendencies and primitive survival, the limbic system *"[...] adds behavioral and psychological resolution to all of the emotions and specifically mediates the social emotions such as separation distress/social bonding, playfulness, and maternal nurturance"* (ibid., p. 43).

Panksepp (2006) called these limbic-based networks the *blue-ribbon emotions*, for their ability to organize identifiable affective states, each with predictable behavior patterns. Collectively, these primary effects ensure social-emotional bonding, also known as attachment. To take one example, in a rat, a human, or a horse the PLAY neural circuit, when stimulated electronically, generates both the feeling of playfulness and the interactive behaviors known as play signals. Panksepp denotes each neural circuit proper by writing it in all capital letters, e.g. PLAY, FEAR, etc. I will do the same throughout this paper. Table 1 shows how the neural circuits are associated with domains of affective functioning in the HEAL Six Key Model.

Humans have the largest neocortex of the entire animal kingdom, which is a significant difference from our animal brethren. Yet, our vast cortical powers often fail to help us understand and treat emotional problems. Many human emotional disorders arise within the non-rational, action-imperative circuits of the brainstem and limbic system. These bottom-up affective states, with the potential to overwhelm logic and training, serve a powerful evolutionary imperative: attachment.

Attachment, the glue that keeps a herd together, is mediated by the CARE neural circuit. Epitomized in maternal devotion, attachment experiences and resulting chemistries form the basis for social learning and adult social competence in animals and humans (Panksepp, 2012, p. 284) In his previous work, Panksepp notes that *"Prey species are typically born rather mobile, so they can run away from predatory dangers soon after birth... out of sheer necessity, mothers and infants must bond rapidly"* (Panksepp, 1998, p. 248). Rapid bonding seems to endure in mature equine social relationships, where deep friendships between horses can form very quickly. This is to our advantage in EFPL, where horses quickly form a bond with clients.

*Panksepp's work allows us to see the horse as a fellow mammal who, like us, is impelled* by a neuro-biological imperative to bond and to join, a *highly social mammal.* Animal scientist Temple Grandin points out that, *"The horse's sociability – made it an animal that could be domesticated in the first place"* (Grandin, 2009, p. 119). She goes on to point out that family-based bands of wild horses occupy overlapping home ranges, thus interacting frequently with other small bands in their region. This endows horses with a natural ability to recognize and remember countless individuals for a long time.

Terms like "herd-bound" or "barn sour" were traditionally used to describe the panic of a horse separated from his herd; today we know that deepening trust in the human handler through positive and supportive training is the best medicine for this horsemanship challenge. Even for a trained horse, being led away from the herd may stimulate at least a little nervousness, and he will look to his handler for regulation – not by domination, but "soft leadership" consisting of clarity, reassurance *and confirmation of safety.* This is the basis for a HEAL exercise, "learning to calm a nervous horse".

The so-called pecking order or dominance hierarchy is a strong force in the equine psyche. This expression of herd structure is complementary to attachment and CARE. We explore this dynamic aspect of equine social structure through our Key Four (Yin/Yang balance), guided by Panksepp's research findings on the PLAY neural circuit. Simple activities that depend on one partner being the leader help the client and horse in an exploration of gentle, collaborative "rough and tumble" PLAY. Fortunately, horses *move* rather than *tumble* each other.

The horse's nature as a prey animal is essential to its safety; and it is essential to our client's safety that we educate them about this. Equine senses and instincts are primed to be reactive. Flee first and think later! However, even while in flight a connection to the herd is essential for survival. Horses will run back into a burning stable still occupied by their mates; they will carry their riders into battle under heavy fire. These acts do not show the horse's stupidity, as we may have been told, but the strength of their instinct to bond. Not surprisingly, people take similar actions when those they love are at risk.

In HEAL we also see the horse as a cognitive animal, and a curious one. Curiosity and investigation are hallmarks of the SEEKING circuit, which we see in wild horse bands that typically cover many miles in an average day to satisfy their needs. Activities that involve exercise and exploration (for instance a trail ride or walk in hand) are pleasurable for horses when they are with trusted companions (horse or human). Reward-based clicker training also activates the SEEKING neural circuit. Traditional horse training relies largely on negative reinforcement, which makes it fascinating to observe horses motivated by positive reinforcement. Author Grandin says, *"The clicker has the power to turn on the SEEKING system [the horse] gets to anticipate the reward, which is even better. – [and] it may be the most powerful with high fear prey animals"* (Grandin, 2009, p.129).

The focus of HEAL sessions is the developing partnership between client and horse. The horse is so good at partnering that this can occur in one session under the right conditions, and is even more pronounced over the course of individual therapy. The capacity for empathic attunement is one the horse's greatest strengths, and the horse naturally seeks a person who is able to be present, authentic, and responsive. An important part of the facilitator's role in the EFPL session is to foster a *three-way limbic connection between horse, client and facilitator* (Shambo, 2013, p 14). The horse innately speaks a language of empathetic attunement to feelings; while the human facilitator must be the one to encourage bridge-building to the client's human world. Because of their differing strengths, the horse and human facilitators work together as equal voices within the session, listening to each other with ease and respect. To call the horse a facilitator should not minimize the primary importance of the human EFPL practitioner who is responsible for directing the course of therapy and helping the client build bridges from the relative simplicity of EFPL to the complexities of human life.

## 2.   Theoretical Rationale for HEAL EFPL as Part of Therapy

HEAL's main focus is to support client recovery from complex relational and/or developmental trauma, and related conditions. This was supported by our 2006 pilot study, and follow up qualitative studies with this population (Shambo, 2010 & 2011). Complex PTSD stems from traumatic experiences affecting early development and family life. It is likely to co-occur with other overlapping symptoms. Brainstem "alarm circuits" are chronically overactive, leaving the client vulnerable to unregulated bottom-up affect. Limbic-based attachment and trust templates become distorted, causing many clients to have difficulty navigating the relationship with the human therapist. This is where the horse can help with his naturally simple but immutable instinct to "join" and form a simple and safe bond. In this sense, we employ the horse as a surrogate person, a real relationship where we can access the sub-cortical templates and affective states of the limbic system and brainstem.

The goal of the Six Key Model is for clients to improve functioning in all six affective-relational domains. The domains are explored in a strategic fashion, amplified and brought to life by the process of forming a bond between client and horse (or horses). When the horse is engaged and allowed expression he will reliably show us when the limbic connection becomes stressed, or when he finds the client difficult to understand. Plenty of therapeutic material emerges from working through each present process in a bottom-up fashion, allowing the client to explore and find their own answers with support from the practitioner. Activities vary according to the age, characteristics and needs of the clients, as well as their stage of therapy (see Table 1). The skill sets gained with each key transfer readily to different horses, and are effective in human relationships too (not to minimize that it is more complex with people). The Six Key model serves well for individual short- or long-term therapy, and group formats. Clients with clinically significant issues receive office therapy as well as EFPL, according to need.

EFPL changes the relationship between client and human therapist profoundly, putting them side by side to navigate novel situations bound to arouse the client's old reactions to relational needs, desires and fears. The human therapist brings a plan for the day's session, but the navigation style is bottom-up and flexible. Viewing the horse as a co-facilitator invites the unexpected. The facilitator sets a slow pace and fosters the three-way attunement, providing opportunities for the client's conscious reflection on feelings. The horse participates primarily through proximity, gesture, actions and responses, and body language.

## 3.  EFPL Activities and Strategic Set-Up

All HEAL exercises are framed around natural activities that make up the human-horse relationship, activities that are understandable from the horse's view, including meeting, hanging out with each other at liberty, walking and leading, grooming, and light periods of free play, round pen join up, clicker training, and for some clients, riding. During such activities the horse may be at liberty or handled with a halter/lead or other tack as necessary; and some activities may be in the company of the herd or may be separate.

Rather than asking "what activities do we do in EFPL?", it is more important to ask, what lies behind the choice of activity and how it is implemented for a particular client? Let us take grooming, an activity that most practitioners employ, and look at ways it might be used. Simple grooming, with the horse on a lead, might be chosen for its regulating effect on the client. Grooming is rhythmic, repetitive, relational, and a lovely way for client and horse to become acquainted. This does not mean it is always the best way to spend valuable session time. The practitioner chooses it strategically for a specific benefit. Quiet grooming produces a shared calming state, characteristic of successful emotional regulation and care.

Grooming at liberty can bring up archetypal relationship dilemmas, particularly if the horse moves away, declining to be groomed. Set up this way, it is likely to bring up relationship anxiety, or a cognitive dilemma about whether to pursue the horse or let go of the goal. The practitioner should understand the benefits and risks, in terms of client goals and needs. Grooming with hands (no brushes) makes it much more intimate, opening a door into a profound experience of safe, affectionate touch and skin-to-skin contact. Many of our traumatized clients have deficits in this area, and such contact with the horse can be quite powerful and restorative, safely filling a need that the human therapist could not. It is so powerful, however, that it might be most valuable later in therapy, when the client is ready to revisit and deepen the body-based awareness of Key One.

Equine activities do not become therapeutic exercises without a specific strategy behind them. This guiding strategy determines how the exercise should be set up in order to maximize the chances of therapeutic benefit. This does not mean that the facilitator knows exactly what the horse will do, or how the exercise will turn out. The skilled facilitator knows which issues the client can explore with the activity. Good exercise set-up increases the chance for the horse to provide the client with an emotional correction. This enables a deliberate progression through the Six Keys at a pace and depth appropriate to each client's needs and tolerance, to make progress through the course of therapy.

## 4.  Progression of Therapy in Stages

Table 1 summarizes the function and activities of the horse in HEAL sessions according to stage of therapy. EFPL can provide immediate regulation and a sense of curiosity, possibly even hopefulness. It is natural for a simple bond to form between human and horse. This is not a sentimental bond, though it can be full of feeling. It has practical dimensions: activity, attention and proximity. We give the horse as much liberty as is practical, while providing enough structure to help client and horse feel safe and to guide the process toward treatment goals.

Each client's course of treatment will differ, including different starting points in the Six Key scheme, but ultimately there is wisdom in a gradual progression of the Keys. The exercises in the first stage of therapy focus on affect regulation, sharing space, creating safety, helping the client to stay present and not dissociate, and creating the three-way alliance, client-horse-practitioner. This stage is normally focused around Keys One & Two, and can last from a few to many sessions. This first stage of therapy may not look like much to an observer – two people hanging out with a horse or horses at liberty, eventually engaging in the simplest activities of touching, leading, or grooming. The facilitator slows the action for two important reasons: to match the emotional processing speed of the horse, and to give the client time to sense feelings, to find words, and proceed by her own initiative and what she senses from the horse. This stage is very helpful for calming and de-escalating anxiety.

In the second or middle stage, the client-horse relationship can be taken more deeply with more challenging human-horse exercises that increase the need for regulation and communication between the client and horse. Exercises in Key Three target social anxiety, critical self-talk, identifying incongruence and defensive patterns; Key Four exercises target issues of requesting, assertiveness, sending clear and congruent messages, and collaborative leadership. Key Four is also highly integrating as it is more of an action key. This second stage of therapy is characterized by "the rub" we often experience in relationships – and the client's ability to relieve the rub and find harmony by use of the Keys.

The culmination stage of EFPL emerges from the structure, integration and competency realized in Key Four exercises, which enable the transition to Key Five. This stage is marked by confidence and accomplishment with client and horse as a team in relatively complex tasks. At the same time, the client is being nudged in the direction of risking safe and healthy human connection in her natural community. All the Keys contribute to confidence and to success in Key Six, activation of the CARE neural circuits and improved capacity for social attachments.

## 5.  Glimpses into a Course of Treatment with EFPL

I am a Licensed Clinical Counselor working from a home-based office, on a private ranch where the EFPL takes place. With individual clients I usually work as sole practitioner, as is the case with this client I'll call "Alecia". She was 17 the winter she began therapy. At age 15, she had been raped. Many factors involving involuntary disclosure and ensuing events exacerbated the trauma and affected her life at school with ostracism and bullying. She was currently not attending school, was agoraphobic and had threatened suicide. Despite her frequent panic attacks, she had consented to come because of the "horse therapy". I felt that EFPL would significantly improve the chances of treatment success for this very withdrawn client.

In the first session, I briefly imparted some basic mindfulness skills to get us started, then took Alecia to meet all the horses. They were in separate paddocks, giving her the chance to view them individually, using the concept of mindful awareness. A sorrel mare named Dixsi sparked an interest, and we spent the remainder of this session in her paddock, with Dixsi still at liberty. After a quick greeting sniff, the mare casually cropped grass near the girl, and as she grazed, kept stepping between my new client and me. Though casual, the gesture felt protective. When I mentioned this to Alecia she shrugged and turned away, but I saw her suppress a fragile smile. She put a hand on Dixsi. Thus began our three-way limbic connection.

Alecia had an exaggerated startle reflex, a low tolerance for unexpected events, and was easily triggered into panic attacks. Throughout this first stage of therapy (around three months) we spent a lot of time in regulating activities: walking with Dixsi, brushing her, learning to breathe with her, even gentle body massage for the horse, or just sitting in the pasture. Continuing emphasis on mindfulness and the somatic approach gave Alecia basic skills for modulating anxious arousal and gauging her safety around the horses. Allowing her to hold Dixsi beside her on the lead line helped to regulate the apprehension that constantly plagued her.

For Alecia, a palpable turning point occurred in a session during the early summer. She went to the pasture to fetch Dixsi, and brushed her while we talked about what to do that day. Alecia said she wanted to feel a stronger bond with Dixsi. We untied Dixsi's rope, and I helped Alecia establish a "ground tie", asking Dixsi to voluntarily stay put. After grooming, Alecia built an even stronger connection by synchronizing steps through walk/trot/halt transitions. This exercise builds attunement between client and horse. A sudden rainstorm drove us into the indoor arena. Once in the arena Dixsi could not see the other horses, and she became upset, perhaps because of the storm as well as the separation. She ignored Alecia, who was still trying to lead her, and called to the herd with loud whinnies. Nothing like this had happened between them yet. Alecia's face lost focus, then she dropped Dixsi's rope entirely as a panic attack kindled. I quickly stepped beside her, emitting an audible out-breath, "Sh-h-h-h-h." The horse recognized this calming signal; her gaze returned to us and her body lost its rigid tension. Alecia looked at me, mouth open, the rising panic forgotten. We spent the rest of that session practicing the purposeful use of breath to soothe Dixsi while leading her away from the herd. Alecia showed genuine pride in this, and it signaled a turning point to the middle stage of therapy, where there was more emphasis on mutual regulation in more challenging exercises.

I knew that Alecia would benefit from the robust "join up" exercise used to explore the PLAY neural circuit in Key Four. Alecia was scared of high energy, but gradually accepted the idea that horses benefit from exercise, and she learned to put Dixsi through her paces (the natural horse gaits of walk, trot, and canter) and turns, using voice commands and body language. Dixsi, a spirited Arabian horse, was enthusiastic about the high-energy play. Dixsi's energy would go up, way up, causing Alecia to dissociate, which made Dixsi anxious. Alecia struggled with panic but, with persistence, gained the ability to ground herself and breathe through, an effective signal for the red mare to stop and attune to Alecia with ears pricked. Dixsi became so calm and attached from this exercise that Alecia could lead her around the ranch with just a light neck rope instead of the halter.

Alecia's favorite activity during the culmination stage of therapy was horse dancing with Dixsi. She did this several times, bringing her own music to share with me. By that time she was close to finishing her last year of high school, and she even took expressive dance as an elective. Alecia had been in EFPL therapy (with some office sessions) almost two years. When the time was right we terminated therapy, taking care that she had appropriate support for continued progress.

## 6.  Theoretical Foundations/Resources for HEAL Model Practice

The HEAL model integrates practitioner skill sets based on well-supported theories of treatment for complex PTSD. I will list these along with some of the resources we recommend in HEAL trainings so that readers may explore on their own.

One of the most important theoretical foundations of the HEAL model is mindfulness. Horses are exquisitely sensitive to the breath and other markers of our biological arousal, including the relationship of thoughts to our energy system. The commitment to mindful awareness, and mindfulness practice, permeates HEAL EFPL throughout all exercises and Keys. There are many good books and one of our favorites is *The Mindful Therapist* (Siegel, 2010).

Models of somatic therapy elaborate on and enhance mindfulness, plus they have well-established value in trauma therapy. *Waking the Tiger* (Levine, 1997), and *Trauma and the Body* (Ogden, Minton and Pain, 2006) are wonderful resources for the EFPL practitioner. Babette Rothschild's classic work *The Body Remembers* (2000) is a wonderful resource for trauma work in general, quite relevant to EFPL with its emphasis on titrating arousal and on boundaries. The cognitive model is helpful in the integration of top-down and bottom-up processes; and also because horses do appear sensitive to humans' thoughts, probably through their immediate effect on our nervous systems. We also want practitioners to understand attachment theory. The volume *Healing Trauma: Attachment, Mind, Body and Brain* (Solomon and Siegel, eds., 2003), features the work of leading researchers and clinical theorists in the field of trauma treatment. Panksepp's prolific works remain the best source for information on each Key/neural circuit.

## 7.  Assessing the Well-Being of Therapy Horses

Temple Grandin, in her book *Animals Make Us Human*, relies on the work of Panksepp to establish principles for animal emotional welfare across all species. *"The rule is simple,"* says Grandin, *"Don't stimulate RAGE, FEAR, and PANIC, if you can help it, and do stimulate SEEKING and PLAY"* (Grandin, 2009, p. 23). For highly social mammals, engagement of the CARE neural circuits is essential too. Without sufficient CARE opportunities, depression and anxiety are inevitable (Panksepp, 1998, p. 263). Here is a Six Key assessment of therapy horse well-being.

- *Key One:* Considering work, rest, and social time, does your horse exhibit anxiety or stress (for example, fidgeting or avoidance); or depression (lack of interest, low activity)? Does he show willingness and engagement for his work in EFPL? Does your horse have adequate work-rest balance?

- *Key Two:* Do you allow your horse to express boundaries and signal his needs in interactions with humans? Does he respond to boundary signals with respect? Have injuries occurred in human-horse interactions? Boundaries are like a garden, healthy ones need maintenance! *"Confidence breeds respect and vice versa.... A common mistake is too much "snuggling up" to a horse from the beginning"* (Delgado and Pignon, 2009, p.118).

- *Key Three:* Are you able to see a horse's misbehavior as communication? How can you tell if the horse has confidence in the tasks required of him? When your horse "leads" the session, can you read what he is saying? Learn his language. *"The horse makes signals with every part of his body. I have to learn to read his thoughts by watching his nostrils, his ears, his eyes, his general attitude. He is telling me with subtle signals how he feels"* (Delgado and Pignon, 2009, p. 94).

- *Key Four:* Where is your horse in the pecking order? Where are you in relation to him? What are your play signals with the horse? Does your horse get adequate exercise for his age and physical condition? Sharing exuberant social play helps horses recover from a heavy EFPL session. PLAY promotes integration of body, mind and spirit in joyful expression. For EFPL, soften the training aspect of horse activities. Make it relational and give the horse more room to volunteer, lead and teach.

- *Key Five:* How do you encourage your horse's intelligence and continued growth? Do you use reward-based training? Shared opportunities to explore and learn new things help mammals build strong bonds. *"I have experienced that horses who do not normally get along with each other will buddy up and become friends if they travel together,"* says Linda Tellington-Jones (2016, location 217/972)

- *Key Six:* How does your horse express his care for you? What is his role in the herd? Does he "take on" emotions from humans (for example, a tendency to colic after intense sessions)? A strong partnership is characterized by taking care of each other in practical ways. *"The confidence I have in my horse is about the same as the confidence the horse will have in me. We both have to earn it"* (Delgado and Pignon, 2009, p.160).

The best pathway for EFPL practitioners to understand the equine mind is to spend a lot of time observing, or even living with, a sizable herd (upwards of 8 horses of mixed age and gender). I have served in many roles during my horse-focused career: instructor, trainer, wilderness guide/ packer, farrier, and EFPL Facilitator. I have learned the most about horses as social animals by caring for large herds under natural conditions (lots of shared turnout). Their attunement to each other makes them one body, like a flock of birds or a pod of dolphins. Still, they are uniquely accessible to us, willing to let us in, gifting us with their individual needs, quirks, and intelligence. They reveal to us our own nature as mammals that bond, highly social mammals that also want safety and mammals that thrive in the caring shelter of one another.

**About the Author**

Leigh Shambo, MSW, LPCC, founder and director of Human-Equine Alliances for Learning (HEAL). When her life was touched by injury and loss in 1988, horse trainer and equestrian coach Leigh Shambo found that the horses she once focused on as athletes became participants in her recovery. Learning natural, non-coercive training techniques, Leigh saw her own process of emotional healing mirrored in the emotional responsiveness of horses. Similar to humans with their instinct to bond, need for safety, and highly social nature, horses make wonderful teachers for humans seeking better relationships. Leigh started HEAL as a small collective of interested MH therapists and horse educators in 2000, after completing her Master's Degree in Social Work and gaining credential as a Mental Health Counselor. HEAL's organizational mission is to support and promote equine-facilitated psychotherapy through HEAL-sponsored research, education and direct service. Along with developing HEAL, Leigh has been in private practice for over 15 years, helping individuals and families resolve past trauma and grief to cope with current life challenges through office-based therapy and equine therapy. HEAL has grown, offering training programs in the US and other countries. Leigh is author of *The Listening Heart: Limbic Path Beyond Office Therapy* (2013), describing the HEAL Model of equine mental health and learning for humans of all ages.

## References


Delgado, M. and Pignon, F. (2009). *Gallop to Freedom: Training Horses with the Founding Stars of Cavalia*. North Pomfret, VT: Trafalgar Square Books.

Grandin, T., and Johnson, C. (2009). *Animals Make Us Human: Creating the Best Life For Animals*. FL: Houghton Mifflin Harcourt Publishing.

Levine, P. (1997). *Waking the Tiger: Healing Trauma*. Berkeley, CA: North Atlantic Books.

Ogden, P., Minton, K. and Pain, C. (2006). *Trauma and the Body: a Sensorimotor Approach to Psychotherapy*. New York: W. W. Norton & Company.

Panksepp, J. (1998). *Affective Neuroscience: the foundations of human and animal emotions*. New York: Oxford University Press.

Panksepp, J. (2006). The core emotional systems of the men mammalian brain: the fundamental substrates of human emotions. In J. Courigall, H. Payne, & H. Wilkinson (Eds.). *About a Body: working with the embodied mind and psychotherapy*. (pp. 14 - 32). Hove, UK & NYC: Routledge.

Panksepp, J., and Biven, L. (2012). *The Archaeology Of Mind: Neuroevolutionary Origins Of Human Emotions*. New York: W. W. Norton & Company.

Panksepp, Jaak. (2012). Keynote address at Clicker Expo Portland 2012, Portland, OR

Siegel, D. (2010). *The Mindful Therapist: A Clinician's guide to Mindsight and Neural Integration*. NY: W. W. Norton & Company.

Shambo, L., (2013). *The Listening Heart: the limbic path beyond office therapy*. Chehalis, WA: Human-Equine Alliances for Learning.

Shambo, L. (2010). A Pilot Study On Equine Facilitated Psychotherapy For Trauma Related Disorders. *Scientific and Educational Journal of Therapeutic Riding; Annual Pub. of the Federation of Horses in Education and Therapy International*, A. I. S. B. L.

Shambo, L. (2011). The HEAL Model Of Equine Facilitated Psychotherapy And Learning. *Scientific and Educational Journal of Therapeutic Riding; Annual Publication of the Federation of Horses in Education and Therapy International*, A. I. S. B. L.

Solomon, M. and Siegel, D., Ed.'s. (2003). *Healing Trauma: Attachment, Mind, Body and Brain*. NY: W. W. Norton & Company.

Tellington-Jones, L. and Lang, C. (2016). *Six Macaques: A Story of Transformation from Lab. Primates to Animal Ambassadors*. Kindle Unlimited, Amazon.com.

CHAPTER 19

# The Human-Equine Relational Development (HERD) Approach

## Incorporating Equines in the Psychotherapeutic Process

Veronica Lac

*This article introduces the Human-Equine Relational Development (HERD) Approach as a foundation within the psychotherapeutic and/or learning process. The HERD approach is based on Existential-Humanistic psychology and Gestalt psychotherapy principles, and places our equine partners at the heart of the process. The emphasis is on supporting clients to build authentic relationships with the horse(s), and to allow them to make meaning of their experiences without interpretation from the practitioner. Through the use of a case example, this article takes a closer look at what that means for both our clients and our equine partners, and the theoretical lens through which we practice.*

The HERD approach is formed through a coherent philosophical and theoretical foundation, where the philosophical concepts influence the emergence of theory and its application. This leads to a consistent approach rather than a mixed bag of tools and provides a truly integrative experience for clients. The HERD approach subscribes to the view that all animals are sentient beings in their own right, and that humans, as animals, exist in relationship with all other animals. In philosophical terms, the *Umwelt* of animal existence (Merleau-Ponty, 2002), or our species-specific ways of being-in-the-world, is seen as the self-organizing principle guiding the animal's behavior and physicality, i.e. what makes us human and what makes a horse a horse (Lac, 2017); which leads to a co-created endeavor between humans and horses that is bidirectional in nature. Thus, the Human-Equine Relational Development (HERD) approach is one that focuses on the ever-evolving nature of the relationship between the two species of horse and human, but also the particulars of any specific interaction between horse and human in the context of equine-facilitated psychotherapy and learning (EFPL). The HERD approach views the horse as a co-facilitator in the therapeutic process, but also acknowledges the responsibility of the practitioners as the guardians of their horses' safety and welfare. This translates into a way of working with horses in a therapeutic and learning environment that places the welfare of the horse(s) in equal standing with that of the client(s).

In a nutshell, the principles behind the HERD approach are rooted in Existential-humanistic psychology and Gestalt psychotherapy, and is based on the three tenets of what I like to refer to as: The here-and-now; What and How; and I and Thou (Lac, 2017). The here-and-now refers to our ability to remain in the present moment in a fully embodied way. This includes not only our awareness of what we are thinking, but also what we are feeling in our body through all of our senses. It also incorporates what our intuitive feelings in each moment might be. What and How refers to the process by which the practitioner holds a sense of curiosity about what is unfolding in the relationship between the client and the horse(s), without jumping to our own interpretations, but simply reflecting back our observations to our clients, and allowing them to make meaning of this themselves. With regard to the welfare of our equine partners, this means paying attention to the most subtle of movements and behaviors as they interact with our clients. I and Thou refers to the philosophical concept of Martin Buber (1958), who distinguishes between an immersive experience of being with another versus an objectified relationship. Holding an I-Thou attitude supports us to be able to become more attuned with the present moment within the relationship, and acknowledge that one cannot avoid making an impact on, or being impacted by, others.

The HERD approach to EFPL is applicable to working with individuals, couples, families, and groups. It has been an effective way of working with clients suffering from eating disorders, trauma, addiction, and attachment disorders. The practitioner may work with equine support staff, but is also trained as an equine professional to ensure that the process can be held in a unified way. The HERD approach incorporates both groundwork and mounted work, and views the relationship between practitioner and equines as a partnership.

Within any partnership, it is important that there is a balance in terms of individual versus collective needs. Healthy relationships need clear boundaries and operate on mutual understanding, compassion, and consideration for the other's welfare. How do we balance our own needs with those of our partner? In the context of EFPL work, it is important that we consider how we meet the needs of our clients without it being at the expense of our horses. The HERD approach emphasizes the importance of being able to differentiate between the practitioner's own projective process and/or confluence with the client and horses in order to focus on the horses' needs. It also calls attention to the client's process of projection and/or confluence with the horse, and the impact this has on the client's ability to relate authentically. Projection in this instance is taken as the process of ascribing aspects of our self onto another rather than taking ownership of it (Philippson, 2001). The term "confluence" comes from Gestalt therapy theory, and refers to the process by which we lose a sense of our boundaries so that we become merged with the other (Polster & Polster, 1974). Neither of these processes is negative in themselves; it is the lack of awareness of the processes that creates challenges. In the process of projection and/or confluence, we become blinded by our own unacknowledged needs and lose sight of the authenticity within the relationship. In both instances, the "other" (be they horse or human) in the relationship becomes part of our own reflected emotions, or merged with our own desires, so that we are, in effect, relating with our self and not the "other" in the relationship. The challenge for the practitioner is to support clients in recognizing this process in-situ in order to facilitate change.

Briefly, the HERD approach to EFP consists of a 5-stage model: Sharing Space, Release and Expand, Deepening, Coming Home to Relationships, and Integration (Lac, 2017). Throughout each session, the practitioner focuses on the client's and the horse's process through these stages. Sharing space refers to the beginnings of the process where the practitioner tracks the way that the clients and horses start to acknowledge the other's presence. It focuses on breathing and being in the moment. Release and expand refers to the way in which both horses and humans move into/out of relationship in a dance of releasing expectations/constrictions, and allowing for an expansion of a sense of self, either physically or psychologically. Deepening is the stage where authentic connection begins to occur, where clients are able to stay with whatever is unfolding between them and the horse(s). Coming home to relationship refers to those moments where clients can sink into the relationship and linger for a while, and begin to (re)discover an authentic way of being. Finally, integration allows for clients to take the embodied experience with the horses and translate that into something they can recognize in their every day lives.

The following case study highlights the HERD approach when working with horses as one of authentic relating. Following the principles of here-and-now, what and how, and I and Thou, the case study outlines the moments when connections were made between the clients and horses, and when they missed each other in the process.

Ben and Marie were referred to me for couple's therapy through a family therapy service. The agency had been working in a family setting with them and their 14 year-old daughter. Their family therapist felt that it would be beneficial for them to attend a series of EFP sessions with me to focus on their partnership. Marie had recently revealed to the family therapist via email that she had experienced some childhood sexual trauma that she was reluctant to talk about during family therapy.

In the assessment process, Ben voiced frustration that he felt isolated in the family process. He explained that however much he tried to engage in family matters, Marie would sidestep his attempts to become involved. Marie explained that each time Ben tried to intervene, she would feel criticized in how she was handling the situation with their daughter. They both agreed that they needed some help to reconnect with each other. Their presenting issue in family therapy was their teenage daughter's struggle with bulimia nervosa. Ben and Marie recognized how their daughter's illness had impacted the relationships within the family, but were also aware that the ruptures were not all because of her illness. Ben had also recently been made aware of Marie's trauma history, but did not know the details. After going through the HERD safety protocol, I invited Ben and Marie to enter the paddock to meet and greet the horses. It was a bright, sunny day, and the horses were peacefully grazing in the paddock. They were standing close together near one corner of the field, with their backs to us as we entered. As the couple approached, one of the mares swiveled an ear towards them, picked up her head, and trotted towards the opposite side of the field. She was quickly followed by her two herd members. Once there, they dropped their heads and resumed their grazing. Ben and Marie stopped in their tracks and turned towards the herd once more. Once more, they began their approach. Once more, the mare swiveled her ear, picked up her head, and trotted away. The other two horses followed. The couple stopped and turned towards the herd. I asked them to describe their experience so far. Ben said that he was feeling disappointed that the horses didn't want to engage with him. Marie said that she felt they didn't want to be disturbed, and wanted to wait to see if they would come to her.

Me: How do these feelings show up in your relationship?

Ben: Oh, all the time. I'm constantly feeling like she doesn't want anything to do with me.

Marie: That's not true! Of course I want you to be involved. I just don't know how to let you in.

Marie's shoulders slumped, and she looked down at the ground and became tearful. "I know it's not fair on you. I just don't know how to let go", she said. "I wish you'd let me help," said Ben.

This interaction created some palpable tension between them, and I noticed the horses had moved further away. Wanting the couple to explore how they shared space with each other, I invited them to take a few moments and observe the herd and to choose a horse that they would like to work with together. After a brief discussion, they pointed to Reba, the chestnut mare who had led the others to walk away. Reminding them to pay attention to the themes of inclusion and letting go, I asked them to go and spend some time with Reba.

As the couple approached her, Reba picked her head up from grazing and stood with her ears pointing towards them, and remained in place. Marie stopped about 10 feet away from her, while Ben continued to walk right up to Reba's side. Reba shifted her weight away from Ben but continued to stand in place. As Ben reached up to stroke her face, Reba took a few steps sideways away from him and turned her head away. Meanwhile, Marie had been approached by the other mare in the herd, Cheyenne, who had started nudging her on the arm with her muzzle. As Reba continued to sidestep away from Ben, Marie began to sidestep away from Cheyenne, moving closer to Ben.

Me: I noticed that Reba stood with you until you reached up to stroke her face.

Ben: Yes, she did. I thought because she was staying with me I could ask her for more.

Me: What would it be like for you to focus on being with her at a level that she is comfortable with?

Ben: I don't know. I'm not sure I would be able to tell what she's comfortable with. I guess I was focusing on what I wanted from her.

Marie: I would think that if she moved away, it would be a good indication that it was too much?

At this, I turned to Marie.

Me: What's happening for you right now?

Marie: Well the horses seem to have cornered us and I'm feeling a little overwhelmed.

Me: Where would you feel more comfortable?

Marie: (Taking a few steps away from the horses and Ben). This is better.

I asked if they would be willing to explore their sense of boundaries with a game involving hula-hoops. Retrieving the hula-hoops from outside the paddock where I had placed them earlier, I gave one to each of them. Immediately, Marie put the hula-hoop around her waist and held onto it like a swim ring. Ben held onto his at arms length and twirled it in his hands. I asked them to approach the herd together with the hula-hoops, paying attention to how the horses responded to them, and to what emotions might emerge for them. Ben began by approaching Reba, holding out the hula-hoop for her to sniff. Reba stretched out her neck towards him and grabbed the hula-hoop with her teeth. They proceeded to play a game of tug before they both let go. Ben laughed and picked up the hoop and continued the game with Reba. Meanwhile, Marie had approached Cheyenne, still with the hula-hoop around herself. Cheyenne backed away from her a few steps, and Marie stopped. She stood for a while with the hula-hoop around her, watching Cheyenne. After a while, she dropped the hula-hoop onto the ground, still standing inside the hoop, looked around and watched Ben playing with Reba. Cheyenne took a few steps towards her, but stayed just out of reach. Marie took a step forward, still inside the hoop, and reached out to stroke Cheyenne, who responded by lifting her neck up and closing her eyes. Marie proceeded to scratch Cheyenne's neck.

Watching this unfold, I was acutely aware of my own responses. I was surprised that Reba had responded to Ben with her tug-of-war, as she was usually terrified of the hula-hoop. I was equally surprised by Cheyenne's reactions as she was usually unfazed by any arena props. Having worked in a therapeutic riding environment, Cheyenne was accustomed to a wide range of scenarios, toys, and sensations. The contrast between their habitual behaviors and what was happening in the moment with the two mares intrigued me. I put these thoughts aside and focused on the process unfolding before me. I asked Ben and Marie to describe what they were experiencing in the moment.

Marie expressed delight in her contact with Cheyenne, experiencing her as being respectful of her boundaries while they got to know each other. She felt safe inside her hula-hoop. Ben said he had enjoyed his game with Reba, but also realized that he had been playing a tug-of-war of sorts with Marie, which wasn't so enjoyable. In his desire to support her through her trauma, he hadn't considered how invasive it was for Marie.

Ben: It's like I want to be inside your hoop with you. But I can see that's too much for you now.

Marie: Yes, that would be too overwhelming for me, and doesn't give me space to breathe.

As we talked, Reba walked towards us and stood in between Ben and Marie. Cheyenne walked away and resumed grazing. Marie expressed disappointment that Cheyenne had left, as she was hoping that she would want some more attention from her. "This is what confuses me!" said Ben. "When you get attention, you don't want it. When the attention isn't there, that's when you crave it. Cheyenne was giving you attention earlier and you backed away, but now that she walks away, you want her back. And Reba's right here, but you haven't noticed. It's like whenever I show that I'm there for you, you don't acknowledge it, and focus on what's missing instead. I wish it wasn't so complicated."

We spent a few minutes processing the meaning that Ben had made of their interactions with the horses, with Marie acknowledging that she found it difficult to take in support when it was available, while simultaneously yearning for it. For Ben, witnessing Marie's struggle with taking in support and connection allowed him to gain a better understanding of the process between them. His own tug-of-war with the hula-hoop with Reba signified his responses to Marie's ambivalent attachment process.

Reba had stayed by their side throughout the conversation. I invited the couple to experiment with playing with Reba together, to find a way to connect with each other. Standing in front of Reba, Ben picked up the hula-hoop held it vertically towards Marie. She responded by holding the other side of the hoop. Together, they approached Reba. I held my breath, convinced that she would run away from the hoop. Instead, she dipped her head and stuck her head through the hoop so that it lay on her neck. Ben and Marie were now on either side of Reba. They turned to face forwards. Still holding onto the hoop, with Reba in between them, they began to walk around the paddock. When they had completed one loop around the paddock, I asked them to stop and check-in with what they were experiencing. Once they stopped, I asked them to remove the hula-hoop from Reba. They did, and she stayed standing between them.

Ben: I feel like I have a better sense of how to respect Marie's space.

Marie: I liked being able to feel your presence, but not feel overwhelmed. Really though, I can't believe Reba let us do that with her! I shared with them my surprise at Reba's response, and how she habitually shies away from any of the arena props. Marie began to cry.

Marie: I feel like for her to trust us with the hula-hoop must've gone against all her instincts. I feel honored that she chose to do that. Makes me realize it might be possible to let Ben in and take that risk.

This session marked the beginning of Ben and Marie's journey towards understanding how to connect with each other by attuning to the other's availability for contact in each moment. In subsequent sessions, we worked on identifying more clearly Marie's ambivalent attachment process, in contrast to Ben's need for confluence within the relationship. Reba was a constant companion on their journey, offering herself willingly to work with them in each session.

This case study demonstrates the different stages of the HERD approach. From the beginning moments of negotiating how to share space with the herd and each other, Ben and Marie were supported to gain a clearer sense of what they needed individually and collectively. This allowed them to move into a space where they could release and expand; release from their long held restrictions and rigidity, and open up to an expanded way of relating to each other. This was further deepened by the experiment with the hula-hoops with the horses, before coming to a place where they felt more at home in themselves and in the relationship. They were able to then reflect on the process and integrate their experience in a way that had meaning for them in their everyday lives.

This case study also highlights the importance of trusting the herd's ability to self-regulate. While Ben and Marie were moving through the 5-stages, the herd was also doing this. Working at liberty, they are given the choice to participate in sessions or not. At each moment, they have the freedom to disengage with the process if they so wish. This session demonstrated the importance of allowing the horses to volunteer in this way rather than the practitioner assuming a set of responses from the horse. Reba's willingness to facilitate Ben and Marie's connection through overcoming her fear of the hula-hoop became part of the process. Later on in the journey, we returned to reflect on this first session of how Reba had interacted with them and the hoop. Marie was able to link that to her own process of overcoming her fear of confiding in Ben more about her trauma history. In attending to the horses' needs, allowing time before and after each session for the herd to recalibrate and release is critical. It is imperative that the practitioner is familiar with the horses involved in the session in order to track their habitual ways of releasing tension from the work. At the end of every client session, Reba will roll, snort, and run around the paddock for a couple of minutes before settling back down to graze. Cheyenne, on the other hand, releases by rolling and then lying down for a nap. Consistent with the philosophical and theoretical roots of the HERD approach to EFPL, the herd's welfare becomes part of the relational process. In conclusion, the HERD approach to EFPL prioritizes the human-horse relationship as one of authentic meeting. The present moment awareness of the emerging process between horse and human allows clients to gain an embodied experience of the relationship. Focusing on the horses' responses to the clients allows the practitioner to keep track of the horses' welfare during and after each session. In this way, we can honor the willing partnership that is offered by our equine co-facilitators, while also attending to the client's process.

## About the Author

Veronica Lac, PhD, LPC is the Executive Director and Founder of The HERD Institute offering EFPL training to mental health practitioners, coaches, and educators. Veronica holds a Master's in Gestalt Psychotherapy and a Master's in Training and Performance Management. Specializing in working with eating disorders, trauma, and attachment, Veronica has also developed equine and canine assisted programs for at-risk adolescents in collaboration with residential treatment centers and eating disorder clinics. She is also a PATH registered therapeutic riding instructor. Veronica is passionate about training EFPL practitioners and research in the field of equine facilitated psychotherapy. Veronica is from the United Kingdom and currently lives in Ohio, USA, and brings her multi-cultural perspective to her work.

## References


Buber, M. (1958). *I and Thou.* (R.G. Smith, Trans.). New York, NY: Charles Scribner & Sons.

Lac, V. (2017) *Equine-facilitated psychotherapy and learning: The human-equine relational development (HERD) approach.* San Diego, CA: Academic Press.

Merleau-Ponty M. (2002). *Phenomenology of perceptions.* (C. Smith, Trans.). New York, NY: Routledge. Originally published 1962

Philippson, P. (2001). *Self in Relation.* Highland, NY: Gestalt Journal Press.

Polster E., & Polster M. (1974). *Gestalt therapy integrated: Contours of theory & practice.* New York, NY: Vintage Books.

CHAPTER 20

# A Sentience-Based Approach to Equine-Facilitated Interactions

## From Theory to Practice:
## Building Professional Partnerships with Horses

Angela Dunning

*My view of horses and my approach to equine-facilitated practice: My entire approach is rooted in a sentience-based, consensual-partnership method. This goes far beyond just the theory of regarding the horse as a sentient being, towards fully developing and integrating a practical methodology which enables us to work effectively at an inter-species level. This methodology continues to evolve on a daily basis both as a result of my equine-facilitated learning practice and also through my relationships and daily care of the horses I work with.*

*My practical approach involves working fully with the horse's intuitive behaviors and suggestions; working at the horse's natural pace and rhythm; allowing freedom of expression of all of the horse's instinctual impulses; seeking the horse's consent; allowing the horse choice throughout, and paying attention to its feedback in each moment. In this approach the horse suggests, shows and leads the process. Therefore, we learn from, and even defer to, the horse much of the time during the client-horse interactions.*

I find that when all of these elements are embedded in our approach then we are able to work in partnership with horses in an effective and respectful way. Equally important, is that this approach ensures we minimize, or better still, potentially avoid altogether, any stress for the horses while we are asking them to work with and support our clients.

In addition, I also feel that partnering with horses requires the human facilitators to make significant shifts within themselves in terms of their level of awareness and consciousness around how they engage with their equine partners. This enables us to move beyond a using approach where the horses are "tools", or a means to an end, towards working with horses on an equal footing and in a partnership. In my experience, this requires significant and continuous self-vigilance to ensure we do not slip back into bad habits whether through time or work pressures, or internal pressures formed by our self-doubts, or the need to uphold a professional role.

## 1.  More on How I View Horses:

I believe that horses are sentient beings in their own right, with feelings, needs and preferences which are fully independent of their human handlers. In addition, I view the horse as fundamentally a herd animal with a high need and propensity for social interaction with others. Safety is their primary innate need at all times, which is maintained through their fight or flight responses to all areas of life. Dynamics within herds, in my experience, are often fluid and inter-changeable depending on circumstances, and horses seem constantly to seek either to assert their own leadership or to look for leadership from another herd member. I regard horses as being highly sensitive mammals who are responsive to everything which is felt and experienced in their immediate environment, such as emotions, energy, physical and physiological states of others – including people.

In addition, from a more spiritual perspective, I view the horse as both a physical and a mythical being with potential for guiding humans to a more deeply connected place within themselves, as well as to a spiritual realm where people can access intuitive and non-ordinary states of consciousness more readily. Horses often appear in people's dreams in both their physical and mythical forms; for example, the mythical creature Pegasus is often reported in dreams about horses.

Further still, at times, I find that interacting with horses can provide a vast amount of metaphorical information to people – where the interaction with horses can glean insights into their own behaviors and patterns through what or who the horse, or the horse's behavior, might represent to them in any moment. However, if we solely regard the horses metaphorically I believe we are in danger of losing sight of the fundamental fact that the horse is also just being a horse. Therefore, I believe that this metaphorical view of horses needs to be used with caution. Otherwise, we can fail to appreciate the individual horse's needs and preferences and may then revert to using them for our own or our client's benefit.

## 2.   My Theoretical Approach

### Partnering with horses to support people's growth

I employ an educational and coaching model, significantly informed by the Eponaquest Approach, combined with a range of other coaching, psycho-spiritual and somatic/ mind-body tools. Somatic and body-focused work is at the core of my approach to help participants reconnect to their own body, and to facilitate an inner state in the person which, in my experience, naturally encourages the horses to choose to engage with the person. Creating these conducive *inner-states* also seems to result in a less stressful environment and experience for the horses, and therefore contributes to maintaining their well-being in our work together.

To achieve this, I particularly focus on helping clients move their center of awareness and consciousness down into their heart-center and their gut; rather than being purely cognitively-oriented. In addition, using this somatic-based approach enables me to help my clients access their deep-seated emotions, rather than their predominant surface-level, discordant/defensive feelings, or coping strategies. To do this I use variations on the Eponaquest® method "The Body Scan", in combination with building emotional intelligence skills by working with emotions as information and accessing the messages behind emotions. This requires both fully *feeling* and *responding* to the emotion in order to move through the emotion effectively. Combining these two techniques gradually enables people to become more connected to their deeper emotions and supports them to feel safe enough to begin to feel their emotions, rather than suppressing or controlling them; two states with which the horses seem to feel very uncomfortable.

My approach involves considerable observational and reflective-type interactions with loose horses, as far as possible, combined with talking to help clients understand and process their feelings, bodily sensations, thoughts and behavior patterns. Some active sessions with the horses are also occasionally employed when deemed helpful, such as leading or moving a loose horse, to enable clients to learn how to combine their new-found awareness of themselves and new skills through *actively* engaging with a horse.

The primary population with whom I work is adult women, usually between the ages of 30-65, who are seeking personal, professional or spiritual growth. A large number of my clients are also horse owners who are seeking an alternative, gentler approach to relating to their horses. Many of my clients regard themselves as Highly Sensitive (HSP), empathic, and intuitive and are often currently dealing with these core traits as a challenge rather than an asset. Some clients with whom I work also have symptoms of depression, anxiety or grief. Most are experiencing significant life changes which usually also necessitate adjusting to considerable internal change. Our work together usually involves navigating both these internal and external changes as well as developing tangible new skills for clients to take away.

In addition, I also support, supervise and train other equine-facilitated professionals to help them develop their skills and practice, and to deepen their practice through incorporating the core elements of my sentience-based and somatic approach to partnering with horses. I am presently offering both post-certification training and continual professional development, and I am in the process of developing an equine facilitators' certification training program based on the curriculum in my recent book *The Horse Leads the Way*.

## 3.  Why I Work with Horses and People

I partner with horses to support people because I find they provide a substantial range of quickly and easily absorbed feedback and lessons that people can greatly benefit from. Being so different from people and, yet, equally being so connection-oriented, plus a long-standing historical relationship between the two species, I believe means that horses are ideally placed to facilitate human development. In addition, on a personal level I have a life-long love, bond and fascination with these incredible animals. This has brought me immense enjoyment as well as substantial personal development and healing.

My principal approach to working with horses to support people, as outlined throughout, centers on my belief that the horses are my co-facilitators and partners. In my view, the horses' main role, through simply being themselves, is to lead, to guide and to show us. I believe it is through following this guidance, the horses' general approach to life, and their feedback, that we can learn significant amounts about ourselves and how we engage with others.

The following specific and unique abilities of horses are the main reasons why I find they are so well suited to this type of learning or therapeutic partnership:

- The instinctive and intuitive nature of horses means that they are finely-tuned to everything in their environment. They bring a heightened level of sensitivity and intuition beyond anything that people can sense. This makes them able to sense the emotional and physical state of a person, as well as the person's intentions. They can also sense beyond the mask or persona being projected much more readily than we can, thereby sensing someone's suppressed emotions, gifts or traumas more quickly than we can. This can provide us with a great deal of information as to the current state of our clients.

- Horses are authentic, uninhibited, instinctual animals from whom, I believe, we socially-conditioned humans can learn huge amounts. Therefore, I find that horses can, through their very nature, help us to return to our more instinctive, natural and authentic way of being. In addition, horses are fully present in each moment which encourages us also to adopt and to hone similar mindful capacities, to improve both our relationships with them and our own well-being and quality of life.

- Due to their size, strength and power, just being physically near to horses can immediately bring us back in touch with our own sense of vulnerability. This can provide us with ample opportunity to become more familiar with the discomfort of feeling vulnerable, and thereby develop greater emotional resilience as a result, instead of only feeling our conditioned responses and defensive behaviors which we have developed to protect ourselves. Horses encourage us not to worry too much about fitting in or being anything other than who we really are deep down inside, and instead to reconnect to our true humanity, including our vulnerability and emotions.

- Finally, I find that horses can also offer humans the opportunity to learn and to develop a wide range of beneficial relationship skills such as connection to one's body, thoughts and feelings; learning to trust others again; learning to receive support from others; how to approach others respectfully; how to set personal boundaries and become aware when we tend to overstep others' boundaries; to develop empathy in our relationships; to access long-lost personal power, and to develop assertive, compassionate leadership abilities.

## 4.  The Horse's Role

The horse's primary role in my equine-facilitated work is, first and foremost, to simply be their natural-selves, within their own herd and field environment, and to behave spontaneously and naturally as individuals and a herd. Their other key roles in my work are to indicate, through their spontaneous feedback, how authentic we are being in each moment, and to demonstrate healthy approaches to forming connections and relationships.

Then, the main way in which I work with the horses is to pay attention to their feedback at all times, through noticing their physical, emotional and energetic feedback responses which change from moment to moment. For example, in a split second, a horse can be happy being stroked and then change to wishing the person to stop: a flick of an ear, or a turn of her head, sometimes very subtly, sometimes very obviously; either way, these cues need to be adhered to in order to honor the horse's sentience.

## 5.  Differing Interpretations of the Horse's Feedback

There are usually two main ways in which the horses' feedback can be interpreted. By far the most widely accepted interpretation is that horses are mirroring the emotional, physiological and energetic state of the people around them, including our clients. However, while I acknowledge that this can sometimes be the case, for me, this is only one aspect of how we can work with horses and understand what might be happening in these interactions. If we only view the horses as mirrors to our clients' states then we run the risk of objectifying the horses rather than seeing them as beings in their own right.

In addition to mirroring, because they are individuals with their own needs, feelings and preferences, horses frequently also *respond* to the person according to the person's emotional, physiological and energetic state. An example of responding might be whether they wish to connect or not with a particular person in that moment. This choice by the horse may be related to the horse's preference in that moment *or* the client's present state. These *responses* from the horses are often where I find valuable information and an immediate indication of both their current desire to connect or not, and also to enable me to get a baseline reading as to how the client may be feeling on that occasion.

To enable all of these natural abilities of the horses to flow, I find that it is vital for the human facilitators partnering with horses to be willing to shift from a position of power over another being and onto a more level playing-field, where the horses are permitted to suggest what might want or need to happen for our clients. In this sense then, the horse leads; and, in my experience, this is often when the maximum learning or healing takes place for clients. We need to be willing and humble enough to accept the offerings of the horses even if this counters what we feel we might want or need to take place, or leaves us feeling exposed and vulnerable. Without full cooperation in this way with our equine colleagues, we cannot create a respectful working partnership. Also, we are in danger of modeling for our clients a disregard for the horse's preferences and needs, thereby preferring control over and compliance from our horses, rather than respecting them through clear, healthy mutual boundaries. The horse's well-being must be paramount throughout and takes precedence over everything else including client satisfaction, meeting session or business outcomes, or the facilitator's needs.

## 6.  Case Examples

**Example 1:**

A typical interaction I facilitate, which I call: "Getting to know myself and others", takes place for all new clients and at the beginning of many sessions. The participant stands in view of a herd of horses, outside the horse's boundary fence. No touching or talking is encouraged. The participant scans his body for notable sensations, pain, tension, pleasurable sensations, and his current feeling-state, while watching what the horses are doing. Sometimes they make notes in a notebook. Meanwhile, I observe closely the horses' responses and feedback, as well as keeping a close eye on the client's body-language and sensing his energetic state.

This initial activity has several purposes and outcomes: It enables the participants to start to focus internally – on their bodies and emotions; it gives them and me a "base-line reading" for their present state; it gives me a lot of initial information from the horses (yet without touching or approaching or working directly with the horses), in order to ascertain how the horses are "reading" this participant on that occasion. Finally, the participants' recollection and understanding of both what took place within themselves and how the horses responded, gives us both a lot of material to use as a starting point to understanding their relationship to themselves at that point, (e.g. how connected or not they are to their body, emotions, thoughts). Also, by discussing with the participants how the horses responded to their presence elicits valuable information about how they presently understand relationship dynamics. Often clients will misinterpret the horses' responses to them. A typical example of such misunderstanding would be: "The horses didn't seem interested in me." Or: "That horse seemed upset by me standing there." Or: "That horse didn't seem to like me." Such comments provide valuable insights into the thought patterns and beliefs they hold about their intrinsic self-value and worth, and how they approach relationships with others and themselves.

My role as facilitator during this process is to observe, to hold space and to support the participant in whichever way needed. What frequently follows this simple yet profoundly valuable exercise is a vast amount of information for the client to reflect on, as well as providing us with a starting point for our work together. Caution must be exercised in terms of body-focused methods with clients who have trauma, active addiction, unresolved grief, or anything similar. Such clients must be dealt with differently and supported greatly, as this quiet, reflective process can be too much too soon, or reveal significant wounds too early in the process, which would then require further immediate support or therapeutic intervention from a specialist in these areas.

The horse's role in this exercise is simply to be its natural self: in the herd and field environment, as far as possible, or turned loose in an outdoor arena. As stated earlier, I view the horses both as acting as themselves and responding to a client, as well as potential mirrors of a participant's feelings or physical state. This varies depending on what is happening for the participant. Sometimes the horses do some very obvious mirroring of emotions, e.g. two horses might become irritable with each other, or they might yawn, or lie down. At other times a horse may respond by walking far away from the participant, unconcerned with connecting to them. I allow the horses to do as they wish, with no interference on my part at all, no equipment and no expectations on the horses. I simply observe and then reflect back to the client what I noticed, if helpful, during our discussion afterwards.

**Example 2:**

A further typical exercise in my practice is when the participant explores the horse's personal space and boundaries, and also learns how to set a boundary to protect himself physically from the horse. The theoretical approach behind this activity is that horses, like people, have a need for personal space and also a need and desire to set boundaries for self-protection. This activity, more than anything else, I find, enables participants clearly and physically to see the horses as sentient beings in their own right, with preferences, needs and choices about their physical space and environment. Once people start to see clearly these choices being employed by the horses, they can shift their entire understanding and approach to horses, and the people and animals in their own life. This provides huge amounts of learning for people and can be an opening into steadily developing more healthy approaches to relationships. Again, the horse's role here is to act naturally. The horses are loose and have freedom of movement and are free to respond to the participant's approach and/or feeling-state. Sometimes the horse approaches the participant – which then requires the client to set a boundary. At other times, the horse maintains its distance and the participant approaches, noticing and responding to the horse's physical cues regarding its layers of personal space and preferences for the approach. Again, the horse is free to respond and move as he likes, thereby employing choice.

My role is to instruct, to coach, to observe, to reflect and to encourage the participant during this exercise. This is a more coaching and educational exercise where I help the participant through clear instructions before and during the process of setting and respecting boundaries. I also coach them to continue to pay attention to their feelings and bodily sensations throughout by reminding them or asking questions as prompts to encourage them to connect to themselves. I also help them become aware of the horse's responses as these can either be very obvious or subtle; yet both are frequently missed or misinterpreted. So again, teaching participants how to read the horse's cues and understand what they are communicating is part of this learning. However, I allow the participant and horse to engage as much as possible on their own, only intervening if safety becomes an issue or to further help the client.

## 7.   How I Ensure the Horses' Welfare and Well-Being

### Before, during and after the human-horse interaction

As outlined so far, my entire approach to equine-facilitated work takes the horses' welfare, well-being, and enjoyment into account throughout and forms the foundation of my work. In addition to my general approach, there are a number of specific practical measures I employ to further ensure their welfare, which I discuss later. However, first I want to concentrate on three interlinking areas which play a large role in ensuring the well-being of horses in our work together. These are: Equine Choice, Consent and Freedom of Movement.

## 8.   Equine Consent & Choice

Equine consent and choice are at the heart of my approach, and, I believe, need to be present throughout our work if we are to maintain good levels of well-being, health and enjoyment in our equine partners. Without these crucial elements we automatically put pressure on our horse to suppress its natural needs, will, and preferences. Imbalances within the horse can then occur as a result of such suppression and this can impact the physical, emotional, or psychological health of the horse, as well as his intrinsic true nature as the individual he is.

I believe it is vital to seek and obtain our horse's consent at every stage of the process in our work. This requires the facilitator(s) to simultaneously pay close attention to and be willing to respond to the horse's movements and feedback in every moment. Therefore, if a horse says no to taking part – either on that day, or in that session, or in a particular activity, then I honor that decision. In my experience, when we do so we are more likely to be able to ensure our horse's well-being *and* we demonstrate to our clients that through listening to the horses we respect them. I feel that in order for us to work in an equal partnership with horses requires the human facilitator(s) to be actively willing to do these two things: listen and honor. This approach, I find, can be cultivated through ongoing self-awareness and professional development on the part of the human facilitators.

The issue of choice is closely linked to the issue of consent yet can manifest in slightly different ways. With consent, we may be asking the horse to participate in something. Whereas with choice, the horses often instigate something with a client, meaning consent is implicit in their desire to engage. In my book, *The Horse Leads the Way: Honoring the True Role of the Horse in Equine Facilitated Practice*, I focus on the horse having choice for the vast majority of the time. However, I do also acknowledge that there are a small number of times when we might need to counter the horse's choice. For example, if safety of the client becomes a factor, or if I feel that a client is needing a certain type of horse to work with and I may gently guide them towards a more suitable horse. For me, however, these are very much the exceptions rather than the rule.

Some of the most common examples of how horses give their consent and employ choice in this work would be: choosing to work with a particular client; choosing not to leave their herd and entering a round-pen, or asking not to be approached or touched.

I also find that employing equine consent and choice brings great benefits to our clients. Enabling choice often creates avenues to explore with clients that I could never think of initiating without the horses' input; so without choice we are at risk of missing vital cues from the horse as to how the session might unfold. Furthermore, if we override the horse's act of consent to participate, we model for our clients an action of controlling another being, or to put it another way: we use the horses for our or the client's benefit. This type of usage or objectification is often a core issue for the very people who seek out equine-involved interventions and so not reinforcing this dynamic with our horses can therefore be vital for our clients to witness. Otherwise it is likely that our clients will leave with little substantial or long-lasting change and possibly a reinforced view of their own lack of value and worth. Therefore, how we treat our horses in our practice also has a direct impact on the final outcomes for our clients; the two are inextricably linked in my experience.

## 9.  Freedom of Movement

Along with choice and consent, freedom of movement is another key factor when working with horses. By nature, horses are essentially nomadic flight or fight animals. This means they constantly move, unless they are resting, and that movement is clearly vital for their survival: they move away from danger wherever possible, or towards danger in order to assess it first. Therefore, to maintain balance of health and well-being in our equine partners, we also need to allow for them to move about freely and naturally as much as possible. As a result, my preference is to work with the horses in their environment, for example, their field, rather than bringing them into an artificial human environment, such as an arena or stable yard to carry out my work. This enables the horses to feel safer and thus more relaxed and happy to engage with us. In addition, it automatically brings us onto a more level playing-field with the horses, and also encourages us and our clients to shift our inner-state into one which means the horses are happy for us to enter their environment. Once the session has begun it is vital that the horses can continue to move about freely and leave, should they wish, by employing choice.

As well as these three key elements, as stated earlier, I pay attention to the horses feedback in every moment, including checking whether they are happy to proceed or not, as this is my main indicator for whether the horse is employing consent or choice. It is also my primary means of honoring them as sentient beings. I also always bear in mind that with some horses their feedback may be less obvious or masked. For example, certain horses may fall into the category of being "very good therapy horses", but this may be because they have a tendency to cooperate or comply too willingly, or even shutdown or dissociate too easily. A quiet horse may not just be quiet; he may be dissociated in order to cope. This may be either through a high degree of dependency on his human handlers or due to learned helplessness, which can definitely compromise the horse's physical, psychological and emotional well-being, particularly over a long-period. Therefore, consent, choice and feedback are all closely interconnected.

In addition to all of the above, and along with the general routine health support for the horses including providing a healthy diet, regular hoof and dental care and all-year round turn-out in a herd, the following are some additional practical measures I undertake daily to support further my equine partners' health and well-being:

- I ensure the horses I work with are healthy and well enough to work on a physical, mental and emotional level. If any illness, imbalance or poor condition is present, I do not work with that horse until it is fully recovered, unless in the exceptional circumstance where a horse clearly indicates its wish to work with a client/s, which he might do through directly approaching or touching the client/s. Sometimes the horse's own healing can come through the process of seemingly "mutual healing", but as always, I allow the horse to make this decision for himself.

- I ensure that the horses' basic needs are always met throughout the session by providing free-range access to food, water, herd mates and shelter.

- I find out about the horses' workload that day/week/month to ensure they have had sufficient time-off from work and are receiving a good work-rest-play balance. For example, I generally would not work with a horse who has just finished another equine-facilitated session, or just been ridden, or competed, etc.

- In addition, no force, coercion, manipulation or dominance is employed in any part of my work, and any physical confinement is kept to a minimum. I use a minimum of equipment (at the very most a head-collar and lead-rope when helpful or necessary, and something to act as a boundary-setting device if required by myself or the client). In addition, I keep task-based activities and exercises, such as obstacle courses, to the bare minimum as I find these can quickly deteriorate into "just an exercise to complete", and can potentially restrict the horse's choices and freedom of movement, as well as diminish the focus on the relationship between client and horse.

- Finally, after and in-between sessions, I employ a wide-range of natural and holistic therapies and remedies to support further the horses and maintain their health naturally as far as possible; as and when they want or need this. This may include any of the following: body-work such as physiotherapy, chiropractic or massage, energy healing, Shamanic healing, homeopathy, supplements, and self-selected herbs and essential oils. I also regularly undertake body and breath-focused meditations with the horses, and sometimes also offer shamanic drumming, to create an ongoing relaxing and re-balancing environment for the horses.

To conclude then, I find that if all of these elements of my approach are employed in my work, along with this regime of daily care of my equine partners, the horses are then happy to support our clients. Therefore, the utmost consideration of the horses and giving them a voice in their work is vital for me and forms the basis of our working partnership.

## About the Author

Angela is an Equine Facilitated Learning (EFL) practitioner who completed the Eponaquest Instructor training with Linda Kohanov and Kathleen Barry Ingram in 2007. She delivers in-depth personal growth programs for adults, mainly women, wishing to heal from a mind-body split, a lack of authentic self-esteem, a lack of self-trust, as well as develop healthier relationship dynamics as taught by the horses. Her approach focuses on embodiment and on developing subtle self-awareness and self-responsibility. Passionate about improving industry standards and the welfare of horses in personal growth and therapeutic interventions, Angela delivers continuing professional development training to practitioners, supervision, mentoring and consultation services. Due to the mounting concern in recent years about some areas of practice and training, in particular where horses were being used as "tools" or peripheral elements of a mainly human-led process, she wrote the recently self-published book, *The Horse Leads the Way: Honoring the True Role of the Horse in Equine Facilitated Practice.*

## References


Kohanov, L. (2001). *The Tao of Equus: A Woman's Journey of Healing and Transformation through the Way of the Horse*. New World Library

Kohanov, L. (2017). *Riding between the Worlds*. New World Library

Dunning, A. (2017). *The Horse Leads the Way: Honoring the True Role of the Horse in Equine Facilitated Practice*. YouCaxton Publications

CHAPTER 21

# The Journey to Healing ...
# Through the Eyes of the Horse

Marlene du Plessis

*"The past is our soul and anchor.*
*Do not let time wash it away.*
*It is our bridge to the present.*
*Do not let ignorance tear it down.*
*And, it forms our guideposts to the future.*
*Do not let fear shred it apart."*

*Jerry Long*

*Humans are created to function within relationships, within a family unit, a community, with friends and peers, nature, a core, and the need to connect with a higher power. The most important relationship is often missed, and that is the relationship with oneself. To truly accept and love oneself, in a non-vain and non-superficial way, is one of the biggest challenges for many. The ability of an individual to develop the capacity to navigate successfully and to experience all the levels and facets of relationships starts just after conception. A scary thought at the best of times!*

Our need to belong, to connect, to communicate, to feel heard, to be accepted and to feel safe, is the very characteristics that makes us vulnerable. Trauma, in any form, destroys relational connections and leaves us with existential distress, the incapability to trust, and eventually causes the inability to form and experience healthy relationships.

Taking the cue from the founder of Logotherapy, Dr. Victor Frankl, a psychiatrist and neurologist, we will start with how the human is neurobiologically wired. How traumatic life events affect the individual and his/her development and functioning; how therapeutic facilitation is received and how it should be delivered for optimal healing.

The fields of neuropsychology, neurobiology, cognitive psychology, neuroscience and counselling, therapy and even life coaching, are extremely wide and complex. It is impossible to cover all the concepts in detail; thus, the author will be touching the basics in neurobiology and how it presents itself in the therapeutic process. It is therefore the purpose of this paper to understand why Logotherapy within the experiential therapeutic methodology of Equine Assisted Therapeutic Facilitation is such a powerful process of healing for the client who experienced trauma, and an equally powerful process of learning to those who want to improve themselves. It all boils down to relational healing and restoring the client's world.

It is important to mention, at this point, that the author acknowledges that in psychology, counseling, and related practices, each discipline has its scope of practice, strengths, and vulnerabilities. It is accepted that each discipline will acknowledge its strengths as well as its limitations. In the end, each form a part of the whole, and there is no reason why they cannot be integrated to the benefit of the client. The words "therapeutic facilitation" will therefore be the composite term used to include all forms of psychological therapy and counseling in its various forms.

## 1.  The Brain, the Body and Behavior

The way we as humans are wired – how we think, feel, and behave – is shaped through various neurobiological systems. Our actions, thoughts, and behaviors, in return, play an important role in the neurobiological wiring of our brain. Although genetics may play a role, human beings become a reflection of the world in which they grow up and develop. If this world is safe, predictable, and characterized by healthy enriched relational and cognitive opportunities, the individual grows to be a self-regulating, thoughtful, and productive member of the family, community and society. The opposite is also true, that if this world is unsafe, chaotic, threatening, and empty of kind words and supportive relationships, an impulsive, aggressive, inattentive individual with difficulties forming any kind of relationship will most likely emerge (Perry, 2004).

To understand human behavior without going into much detail requires us to start at the beginning.

The human brain and nervous system are fascinating and vastly complex structures. Development starts in utero and is especially active and vulnerable during the first four years of life (Perry, 2004). Not only is the brain a complex organ, but it is vulnerable to a large variety of pathologies, many of which are present with psychological behavioral abnormalities; some due to environmental inputs, others due to developmental problems. The brain is comprised of billions of cells called neurons and glial cells (Perry & Hambrick, 2008). They receive information from both external and internal environments and integrate and transmit this information via interlinked complex chains, pathways, and neural networks. Physical connections between neurons – called synaptic connections – increase and strengthen through repetitive use, while those not in use wither away. Therefore, every brain adapts uniquely to the unique set of stimuli and experiences in that individual's world. Early life experiences determine whether genetic potential is expressed, full potential achieved or not (Perry, 2004; du Plessis, 2016; Weiten, 2015; Gilgard, 2012).

The brain facilitates our movements, our senses, our thinking, feeling and behavior. As the brain develops, from bottom to top, the lower less complex and more regulatory systems, the brainstem and diencephalon, develop first (Perry, 2004; Perry & Hambrick, 2008). It controls heart rate, body temperature and other survival-related functions and stores anxiety or arousal states associated with traumatic events. These sections are incapable of conscious perception (Perry & Hambrick, 2008). During the first years, the brain develops outwardly, towards the neocortex, and so the complexity of functions increases (Perry, 2004). The higher parts of the brain become more and more organized and functionally capable as the individual matures, with final major changes happening during late teen and early adulthood.

The limbic system stores the emotional information, also known as the feeling part of the brain. It is made up of the amygdala, the hippocampus, the thalamus, and the hypothalamus. The amygdala is the center for identification of danger. It is the key player in the triggering of the brain's alarm system when there are perceived threats or danger and gives rise to feelings of fear, apprehension, and anxiety, which initiate a stage of alertness. (LeDoux, 1999). The hypothalamus alters the internal feelings to external actions by preparing the body to protect itself resulting in behaviors such as attack, flight, or retreat, freeze or panic (Wilson, 2014). It is a place of no words and no thoughts, only actions.

The neocortex controls abstract thought and cognitive memory. It is known as the thinking part of the brain and is made up of an outer layer consisting of two hemispheres, left and right, joined by the corpus callosum. Each hemisphere is divided into four lobes and is the largest and most complex part of the brain with the lobes dedicated to specific tasks. This part of the brain helps to reason, reflect on experiences and consider various options for responding. It is this part of the brain that enables us to put words to our feelings, to settle ourselves when we are upset, and to make intentional choices (Perry, 2004; Weiten, 2015; du Plessis, 2016).

Optimal brain development happens when the individual experiences consistent, predictable, enriched, and stimulating interactions within attentive and nurturing relationships. Facing new and challenging situations, causing stress and some anxiety, is normal, and, per se, these experiences, when happening within safe and supportive relational structures in place, do not need to be problematic. Within this safe space, they become learning experiences. Moderate and predictable stress triggers moderate activation of stress-responses – something an individual needs to navigate through on life's journey, enabling the forming of strong stress-response capabilities, otherwise known as resilience.

What happens inside the human brain and body, and how it presents on the outside, could be illustrated as follows: children whose parents provide them with safe, sensitive, and responsive care develop neuron pathways that encode expectations that others will also treat them well, and, in this process, these children develop positive self-concepts. In this environment, they will most likely develop capacities for sensitivity towards and caring for others and will encode these capacities in corresponding neuron pathways. They will most likely develop good social skills, be cooperative and persist when tasks challenge them. Sensitive parenting is therefore internalized by the child, and, in return, the child externalizes these attributes in their own actions (Gilgard, 2012; Perry, 2004).

Another important neurobiological system that needs mentioning, and that plays an important role in therapeutic facilitations, is the mirror neuron system (MNS). Mirror neurons play an important part in imitation, empathy, mindreading, and predicting actions (Rossouw, 2013). Using our example above of how children internalize sensitive parenting, we find that children also imitate and internalize how they are treated; and once again, as result, it reflects how they will treat others and conduct themselves in their world (Gilgard, 2012).

When an individual is exposed to any threat, the brain, through the limbic system, activates a set of responses (called adaptive responses) designed to protect the individual and ensure survival. According to Perry (2014) there are two main adaptive styles: the hyperarousal response (fight or flight) or the dissociative response (tuning out) with a combination of the two used during very traumatic events.

Individuals in a state of fear process environmental information very differently than those who are calm and in control. When in a state of calm and control, the higher, more complex parts of the brain process and act on information received. When in a state of fear, the lower, more primitive part of the brain wired for survival intercepts and processes information. As the perceived threat level rises, the less thoughtful the processing becomes and the more reactive the responses become, dominated by emotions and survival instinct (Perry, 2004).

*Why is this important for therapists to know?*

Clients living in repetitive activation of the stress response system (e.g. during abuse) live in a permanent aroused state. This leaves them ill prepared to learn from social, emotional and/or any other life experience as the limbic system short circuits the neo-cortex. They live in the minute, not in the moment. The hyperarousal responses may be displayed as defiance, easily misinterpreted as willful opposition, resistance, and even aggression. Symptoms of hypervigilance, such as panic, anxiety, or increased heart rate are often present. The dissociative response involves avoidance, psychological flight, withdrawing from society and focusing internally. Presented as detached, numb, and even withdrawal into a world of fantasy, they can also be presented with almost robotic compliance, rhythmic self-soothing of faint episodes. Intensity varies with the intensity of trauma experienced (Perry, 2004).

*Why is this important in relation in to the therapeutic facilitation process?*

If we take a picture of a person standing with a scalpel in one hand, and another person lying on an operating table, the neural interpretation via the MNS is in terms of intention – based on the perceived outcome in relation to previous experience. The therapist, greeting a client with a smile, reaching out to shake hands, will mostly be interpreted on the intention perceived – friendly and safe. But in a violated neural system, the smile and reaching out of the hand might be interpreted by the MNS, based on previous experience, as unsafe, instantly preparing the body for flight or fight. In this case, the therapist's intent and the client's MNS activation may not resonate the same response – depending on the neural pathways encoded due to special environmental/social influences experienced by the individual. For therapists, it is important to know that the most significant body of neural pathways is established prenatally and during the first ten months post birth (Rossouw, 2012); that the brain responds on all levels from the most essential survival needs (oxygen, food, water, safety) to the most complex needs such as relaxing with family. If any of these needs on any level are compromised or violated (drugs, trauma, stress, excessive fear) the neural patterns change, encoding general patterns of self-protection over patterns of problem solving (Rossouw, 2012). Being aware thus enables the therapists not only to understand the individual's responses, but also aid in the knowledge on how to facilitate the forming of new patterns where the neural encoding will ensure problem solving pathways are maximized and self-protection pathways minimized.

Neurobiological information is now available as a therapeutic tool in the approach enhancing mental and emotional wellness. Research has proven that the brain is a social entity and an action organ (Rossouw, 2012; Wylie, Unknown) – its wellness depending on the healthy connections made in and with the environment, and therapeutic facilitations foster the microcosms of the new safe and new secure social structure, resulting in the building of new healthy neural pathways (Rossouw, 2012). Perry (2004) reminds us that the brain altered in destructive ways by trauma and neglect can also be altered in reparative, healing ways. Exposing the client repetitively to developmentally appropriate experiences in a safe environment is the key. With adequate repetition, the therapeutic healing process will influence those parts of the brain altered by trauma. Facilitating these pathways of thinking, feeling, behaving, and ultimately being does not happen overnight. The new networks are fragile and relapse to default patterns easily. Time is of the essence, 6-8 weeks for the Hebbian principle of *"neurons that fire together, wire together"* to kick in and embed the new neural pathway (Rossouw, 2013), and then months to strengthen them. The same can be said when neural pathways are no longer activated – the synaptic strength becomes less and eventually the neurons that used to be attached become detached, resulting in less risk of a relapse into the default pattern (Rossouw, 2013). Therefore, the secret is to facilitate enough activation of the new pathways to ensure the shift and replacement of the default pathways. This takes commitment, personal support (mirror neuron effect), a decision to change and regular pathway activation stimulation (homework) - and central to this all, is the therapeutic alliance (Rossouw, 2013; Wong, 2012).

## 2.  Logotherapy

Viktor Frankl's theory and therapy grew out of his experiences in Nazi death camps. Watching who did and did not survive, Frankl concluded that the philosopher Friedrich Nietzsche had it right: *"He who has a WHY to live for can bear with almost any HOW."* (Shantell, 2002, p:18). Frankl noticed that people who had hopes of being reunited with loved ones, or who had projects they felt a need to complete, or who had great faith, tended to have better chances than those who had lost all hope.

Logotherapy includes the whole person, in the context of the whole world. Within this whole there are three dimensions: the soma or body, the psyche or mind, and the spirit or noetic. Within the traditional theories of science and healing, the spiritual dimension is seldom recognized, but takes up a vital position within Logotherapy. *"A psychotherapy which not only recognizes man's spirit, but actually starts from it, may be termed logotherapy. In this connection, logos are intended to signify "the spiritual" and beyond that "the meaning""* (Frankl,1986, xvii).

The noetic dimension is present in all humans regardless of religious or spiritual orientation. The biopsychological dimensions (body and mind) are pre-determined by factors such as genetic influences, past experiences, and new learnings from the environment. The functioning of these two systems is easily interrupted by external and internal factors such as illness, chemical imbalances, or the effects of trauma. Equilibrium is found in these two systems through relaxation (body) and peace of mind (psyche). The noetic dimension is where the search for meaning is burrowed, constantly guiding the human from where he is to where he ought to be. Finding that meaning results in true happiness (Marshall, 2002).

Logotherapy can, therefore, be defined as a therapy through meaning (Wong, 2014; Lucas, 2000, Shantell, 2002). Man, per Frankl, as cited in Wong (2014), is a meaning-seeking and meaning-making creature. It forms the primary motivation of man in life to find meaning behind his experiences and to use that meaning as a driving force for his future. Meaning is unique and specific to all according to their value system, and different meanings and values can be found by different people in the same situation. It is meaning that makes perceived failure tolerable and success fulfilling (Marshall, 2012).

The three fundamental and interconnected tenets of Logotherapy are:

- freedom of will,
- will to meaning
- meaning of life.

Each of these tenets will be discussed briefly.

*Freedom of Will.* Unique to the human. Without freedom of will, we as humans will not have the opportunity to choose how we respond in any given situation. Although this choice can be inhibited by illness or immaturity, the existence of it does not diminish. And choices we make always bear consequences. Thus, freedom is always limited by responsibility (Lucas, 2000).

*Will to Meaning.* The primary motivational force for every individual is to find meaning in experiences, past and present, and to use that meaning as a driving force for the future. Positive life purpose and meaning is associated with strong religious beliefs, membership in groups, and dedication to a cause, life values, and clear goals (Lucas, 2000).

*Meaning of Life.* Frankl, as cited in Shantell (2000, p.20) states *"meaning can be seen as something beyond and ahead of us which draws us out of the narrow and closed circle of total self-concern".* Meaning can be found in even the most miserable and tragic circumstances — it encompasses life as a whole, as well as the specific meaning of an individual's life at any given moment. Fabry, as cited by Wong (2014, p.621) states that *"this individual responsibility is a personal response to ultimate meaning and to the meaning of the moment as they are interpreted by the unique individual".*

It is important to realize that not only internal struggles define meaning in life, but rather how everyone's actions and responsibilities affect and impact those around them. It is the goal of logotherapy to help the client to discover meaning, which already exists. The limits of a client to create meaning will also limit what the therapist can do to determine what is meaningful for the individual. The therapist can only facilitate the answer-seeking process and journey of the client. *"Life is putting its problems to him [man], and it is up to him to respond to these questions by being responsible; he can only answer to life by answering for his life."* (Frankl 2014, p.13).

Lucas (2000, p.12) mentions that the *"very humanness of the human being, such as his values structure or his inherent longing for meaning, must not get lost in the tangles of psychological interpretations – It [Logotherapy] poses the question, as to whether the influence of the human spirit can be turned into practical use toward healing purposes of the other two dimensions"*.

It is in the spiritual or noetic realm that meaning and values are closely related. Neglect of the spiritual quest for meaning and purpose in lives often serves to intensify instead of alleviate suffering, problems and difficulties. Frankl (1986) named it noögenic neurosis, and this state is marked by a sense of "emptiness", of futility, purposelessness and meaninglessness in life, or as Shantell (2000, p.19) says *"trapped in a maze of confusion, people without a meaningful aim or purpose in their lives, are landed in a vicious circle, ending nowhere but in themselves."* This is the direct result of overlooking, and thereby failing to foster, human spirituality, values and meaning in life.

It is this noetic dimension that especially interests therapists, as this is where responsibility towards creativity, authenticity, choices, values, free will, and conscience lies. It is in this dimension that our free will operates, driving us to find meaning in all our circumstances and, ultimately, to find ultimate meaning in life.

Rooted in the dimensional ontology as per Frankl, cited in Marshall (2000), Logotherapy accepts the following qualities of the human spirit, which play an important role during the interaction with the client:

- The spirit is not a substance, but a dynamic.

- The spirit cannot be divided, reduced or duplicated.

- The spirit, as a whole, is greater than the sum of its parts.

- The spirit is the essence of the person, displaying the uniqueness of the individual.

- The spirit is the internal compass or conscience.

- The spirit refers to who we are whereas the body and mind refer to what we have.

- The spirit is not constrained to the here-and-now but spans the past and present and opens to the future.

- The spirit cannot be damaged or destroyed or become ill like the body and mind.

- The spirit expresses itself through the body and mind.

- The spirit may be blocked in certain circumstances such as in immaturity, senility, and illness. These do not, however, change its fundamental existence thereof.

- The spirit is the dimension that rises above and beyond oneself and one's circumstances as influenced by instincts, nature, and nurture.

- The spirit is the source of ultimate freedom.

Accepting the autonomy of the spirit includes respecting it in all humans, even those with psychopathology and dysfunctionality. If the client has the ability to reach within the noetic dimension, and shows a willingness to do so, the client is able to be co-responsible for his/her healing. Unfortunately, the opposite is also true; the client holds the freedom to choose to destroy his/her life. For the therapist, this means that healing can only be supported and not coerced or forced. As Lucas (2000, p.20) states *"one ought to offer help, but not take away accountability."* Lucas continues that in traditional therapy, especially psychotherapy, often the reverse happens. *"Little help is offered, because the therapist strictly works on a non-directive basis or withdraws himself quasi behind an impenetrable wall, without comment. At the same time, much accountability is taken away from the patient because all his difficulties are attributed to internal or external conflicts initiated by others, which labels him as a helpless victim"* (Lucas, 2000; p.20). To rob the human of self-accountability means handing him over to the mercy of fate.

According to Frankl, the individual discovers meaning in life in three different ways which he named values. Firstly, by creating a work or doing a deed, known as the creative value. Secondly, by experiencing something or encountering someone, known as the experiential value (love). Thirdly, by the attitude taken toward the unavoidable, in every situation, at any given time, known as the attitudinal value (responsibility).

Wong (2014), comments that reaching congruency in the quest to live a meaningful life, the individual needs to adhere to the following elements. Firstly, the awareness of everyone's personal purpose and mission in life. Setting goals to fulfill this special mission depends not only on self-knowledge, awareness of talents and interests, but also limitations as well as the influences of external sources such as cultural values, societal norms and religion. Secondly, everyone has gifts and talents that need to be employed in opportunities to fulfill this purpose and mission. However, it will be necessary to develop these innate strengths and gifts. Thirdly, individuals must follow their conscience, their sense of responsibility and accountability to setting life goals and making decisions congruent to their calling or purpose. Logotherapy considers the clients' personal strengths, value systems and understanding of ultimate meaning.

## 3.  Equine Assisted Therapeutic Facilitation: The Theory

Equine Assisted Therapeutic Facilitation draws on a couple of traditional therapeutic modalities. With strong underpinning to Gestalt therapy, Equine Assisted Therapeutic Facilitation entices the principle of assuming that meaning is derived and understood by considering the individual's interpretation of immediate experiences in the present moment (Trotter, 2012). As the client plays an active part in the therapy process, interacting with the natural environment which include the horses, he thus stimulates greater awareness of oneself. From Reality therapy, Equine Assisted Therapeutic Facilitation borrows the principle of the importance of thinking and doing behavior

(Trotter, 2012), which provide opportunity to correlate the present experience into learning a changed behavior. Directive techniques are used skilfully in guiding the client on the journey with the facilitator constantly being aware of the necessity to avoid counter-transference. The principles of action (new) versus insight (change) as well as that of expectancy (disrupting a negative expectation to create a positive expectation or change) are borrowed from Brief therapy where the facilitator may invite or confront the client to grow and to change by creating the context in which change can happen (Trotter, 2012). The Rogerian therapy principles of being client centered, creating an environment where the client can feel safe and unconditionally accepted and encouraging overall congruency, exploring and finding individual solutions, is strongly reflected in Equine Assisted Therapeutic Facilitation.

Elements of cognitive and social cognitive theories are also visible in Equine Assisted Therapeutic Facilitation. Founded on the belief that there is a continuous reciprocal relationship between a person's cognition, behavior and environment, learning appropriate (or inappropriate) behaviors happens through observation. Through the unambiguous and immediate responses to both pleasurable and aversive stimuli, the process to initiate change in existing behavioral patterns, the cause-and-effect principle is commonly found in animal-assisted intervention. The father of the socio-cognitive theory Bandura referred to learning through observation as "modeling" (Fine, 2010).

Stepping outside of the traditional four walls of the indoor office into nature inevitably causes a delicate shift in approach. Being outdoors demands greater client responsiveness, greater self-awareness and focused mindfulness. It also challenges the facilitation team as it is not the perfectly controlled environment of the indoor office. External introjection happens when least expected, creating unique opportunities that influence and change responses and reactions during the sessions. As described by Trotter (2012, p.13) "At times it is counseling in the realm of the unpredictable". Therefore, the Equine Assisted Facilitation space is nothing more than a big sand tray in which the therapy team, horses, and client co-create. The activities given mostly follow the principles of non-directive (client-centered) play during which the client's story unfolds.

As Plato (429-347 B.C.) observed, *"you can discover more about a person in an hour of play than in a year of conversation"*. This process allows the unconscious to express itself in a symbolic, non-verbal way within the, as referred to by play therapists, *"free and protected space"* (Wikipedia®, 2016).

## 4.   Equine Assisted Therapeutic Facilitation – as Experiential Therapy

It is known that traumatic experiences involve most of the senses – sight, hearing, smell, touch – (often physical discomfort or pain) – as well as emotions, speech and thought, and are stored in multiple regions throughout the brain. Since humans are unique, individual, complex beings the experience of trauma is different for everyone although there are basic commonalities (e.g. both affect the biopsychological dimensions) that set this form of suffering apart from mental illness.

Various studies have shown positive results with various populations using animals during therapy. Equine Assisted Therapeutic Facilitation is an innovative, experience-based, and multi-model therapy approach that goes beyond just talking therapy. Talking about a traumatic event or experience can provide crucial information about the client's past and current life experiences. Providing effective therapeutic facilitation must address the here-and-now of the traumatic past, as it is expressed "in the moment", when the reality of human evil surfaces into our client's consciousness. Van der Kolk, cited by Wiley (n.d), states that although talking to clients is vital, fundamentally words cannot integrate the disorganized sensations and action patterns that form the core imprint of trauma. Peter Levine, in his book *In an Unspoken Voice* (2010), systematically explains why therapy needs to integrate the sensations and actions that have become unstuck during the traumatic event. Feelings of powerlessness, the inability to have escaped the event or to stop it happening, all play a significant role in the embedding of trauma.

Apart from trauma clients, effectiveness of experiential therapies is also seen where clients need to work through "unfinished business". Corey (1991), as cited in Klontz et al (2007), defines unfinished business as *"unexpressed feelings that are linked to memories carried into present life in ways that interfere with one's ability to function effectively and remains until an individual deals with the unexpressed feelings.*" It is here that Equine Assisted Therapeutic Facilitation is so powerful. As the client talks, moves, and experiences, with all senses within a safe environment, the event or experience can be altered (metaphorically); this can assist the client to become the master of the outcome of the situation over which the individual previously held no power, and to complete the processing circle of trauma by releasing the emotional charge associated with trauma. Reframing the "illness"(trauma) as an "injury", and recasting its effects such as depression and anxiety as part of the "negative past" that they can replace with a "positive present" and "brighter future" (Milish, 2012) all assist the clients on the journey of ultimate meaning.

## 5.  Why Do We Use Horses?

*"Iberians staunchly maintain that the horse is a gift from God, a gift to help humanity see light and the truth"* (McCormick et al, 2004; p.18) and as legends tell, horses have belonged to the mythical line dating back to the horses of Neptune. Humans subconsciously acknowledge that horses are different from other animals by speaking of a horse as having "spirit" or being spirited. It is the only creature to be mentioned in the Bible as being present in encounters between heaven and earth (II Kings 2:10-12). Being born in humbleness, in a stable, the Lamb of God (the servant) enters Jerusalem on a donkey (Matt 21:7) and the Lion of Judah (the judge) returns on judgement day poised on the back of a white horse (Rev 19:11).

In the world of psychology, we find horses as an archetype in the Jungian collective unconscious mind (universal spirit) portraying both animus and anima qualities. Strength. Beauty. Independence. Power. Gentleness. Kindness. Grace (Kane, 2004). McCormick describes it as follows: *"Experiences with horses can teach us the same lessons we want them to learn: to recognize, contend with, and unify the two sides of our inner nature (the human and the Divine) so that we can ultimately work for a higher purpose"* (McCormick et al, 2004, p.36). Although the author of this paper is cautious regarding mysticism, experiences in the facilitation space make it difficult not to believe that being in the presence of horses, deep-seated memories are triggered, almost primal and vital to our human soul, and the indescribable way horses guide and facilitate the journey of self-discovery and healing during sessions.

On a scientific basis, various studies have proven the enhanced benefits of the human-animal-interaction within the therapeutic set-up (Odendaal, 2002). Perry (2006) as cited in Trotter (2010, p.41) stated that *"beginning the recovery process for relational neglect can start with animals"*. More recent studies have included horses as part of the human-animal interaction equation. These studies confirm that the interaction with horses increases mindfulness (Wach, 2014) thus enforcing the moment-to-moment awareness of thoughts, sensations, feelings, without judgment or anticipation, and the surrounding environment as or Logotherapy defines it, being in the moment. Choosing to participate in a therapy modality that does hold some form of risk is a conscious decision made by the client, exercising free will to choose and, if not the first, another step towards their journey of healing.

DePrekel, as cited in Trotter (2012), argues that working with horses is a very effective approach to clients with attachment issues as equines can provide relational attunement, help the client with self-regulation, and aid in their skills development regarding maintaining internal locus of control. In this process the client is assisted to expand the window of tolerance and to stay grounded and present in the presence of the horse, thus allowing the challenge-by-choice concept, which gives the client mindful experiences leading to opportunities to build new neural pathways.

Reichert, cited by Abbey (2011, p.3), argues that the non-judgmental attribute of horses may be a useful medium in relation to enhancing a *"sense of self-esteem and promoting the expression of feelings"*. Another study by Roth et al, as cited by Abbey (2011, p.3) notes that the interaction with a horse can assist a person in exploring *"feelings, powers of intuition and energy, understandings of self, nature, relationships and communication"*.

Being in the prey rather than predator category, horses' intuitive nature has evolved as a mere function of survival. They are constantly attuned to their surroundings and the subtle communication within the herd as responses to perceived threats and/or an ever-changing environment. In this way, horses have been observed to have acute communication skills within their social structures and highly adaptive behavioral responses.

The horses' ability to sense fear and to interpret human intention as displayed by the human body language and pheromones allow them to respond intuitively to human behavior, resulting in immediate feedback on actions performed (Carlsson, Ranta & Traeen, 2015). They are much more effective and consequent in confronting behavior and attitude than humans (Trotter, 2012). It is this response ability of the horse that creates the opportunities of learning, both cognitively and behaviorally, for the client. It is also the relation to these cues from the horse that provides the therapy team a window into the client's personal world and personality. Through the horse's capacity to reflect non-verbal communication, the facilitation team has the chance to guide the client through awareness and potential (personal) change.

It is safe to assume that horses teach us to appreciate the non-verbal and verbal messages that we, as humans, give to others. They teach us that a relationship requires patience, gentleness, self-confidence, sensitivity, empathy, trust, focus, and keen awareness of especially our emotional tone. They challenge us to take note of our own behavior, thoughts, and feelings and their impact on those around us. They are social animals and within the herd relationships and the abiding expectations that are essential for survival. As horses have different personalities, attitudes, and moods, an approach that works with one horse does not necessarily work with another. On their terms, the participants must earn the horse's respect and trust before imposing their own.

## 6.  How does Equine Assisted Therapeutic Facilitation Work?

The team consists of a group professionally trained and qualified facilitators and therapists using the outdoors and horses as part of the therapy and facilitation sessions. The team strives, through the eyes of the horse(s), to facilitate the clients to discover their own answers and solutions.

Sessions are offered in a facilitation space which consists of a facilitation space/arena or some form of enclosure. The horses are free to move around and interact with the humans in the arena at free will. Although some equipment (e.g. poles, pool noodles, hula-hoops etc.) are supplied, the client may use anything within the facilitation space during activities.

Various types of activities are used basically as a stimulus or starting point during a session. Therefore, each session is experiential, meaning it is not only "talking about it", but "doing it".

In an individual or group session, there is typically an activity with a common, clear goal; for example, the client may be asked to illustrate a specific problem using any or all the equipment. Within the controlled setting of the facilitation space, all work is done on the ground – there is no riding involved and no previous horse knowledge is necessary. In the facilitation space, each horse is constantly, moment by moment, processing information conveyed in the moment by the client, consciously and unconsciously. Feelings, breathing, movement, and posture provide the horse with a catalogue of information, and non-judgmental, observable feedback and responses are immediately offered. Active engagement in activities in an open and honest manner, free of expectation and preconceived ideas, will result in integrating experiences and learning in the moment, transforming "theory" into practice, and awareness into the "right" action.

## 7.   The Best of Two Worlds

**Logotherapeutic Equine Assisted Facilitation (LT-EAF)**

Experiential learning is based on the premise that, by removing the clients from their comfort zone, they can grow and develop through experiencing another perspective on life, their situation, and event. Research confirms that learning happens when the brain perceives the experience as new and different (Perry, 2004; Abbey, 2011). It is not about the activity per se, but the learning that happens as clients discover their own strengths and weaknesses, as well as insights into their own internal resources.

Faced with a challenging situation with which they are unfamiliar, their true, authentic selves tend to emerge. Through the repeated debriefing and probing into each learning experience, clients start to gain some real insight into how and why they behave the way they do, and the consequences of those actions both for themselves and others. The activities with the horses become a metaphor for what is happening in the clients' lives reflecting back information about their personality style, their relationship style, communication ability and team working skills within all areas of their world.

*CR, a 13-year old female, was referred to the facilitation team. She had completed her primary school education and was preparing to move to attending high school the following year. As a sensitive child, this worried her as she felt uncertain and intimidated. CR joined the facilitation team and horses, and during the sessions to follow the journey from primary to high school was created, the possible challenges and fears imitated probing CR to discover her inner strengths and resources in addressing and handling them. Over the sessions, she was transformed from a shy, nervous child to one addressing the challenges with confidence and assertiveness to obtain a positive outcome. CR was able to metaphorically symbolize through the horse she called a "Lion" to move forward from being completely uncooperative to finding complete voluntary cooperation with her requests during the activities.*

From Perry's research (as covered earlier in this paper), we know that the brain is organized in a hierarchical fashion from the least to the most complex areas. The impact of sensitive and responsive parenting, and the forming of healthy attachments has been discussed. Neural networks, the forming and working thereof was briefly touched, discussing the patterns of incoming neural activity forming regulated patterns in normal development and dysregulated patterns when especially early childhood trauma is experienced.

Applying the neurodevelopmental-informed approach as researched by Perry, it is noted that the conventional mental health approach provides experiences that target higher level regions of the brain (mostly talking therapy), while traumatized individuals' problems are related to disorganized or poorly regulated networks originating lower in the brain. Experiential therapy, such as equine assisted therapeutic facilitations, accesses not only the lower part of the brain and can mitigate the damage done by early trauma, neglect, or abuse, but also the right brain where emotions, feeling and experiences are stored without words. Participating in basic equine related activities that include, but are not limited to, grooming, brushing, leading horses etc., will give the client a sense of calm, accomplishment, comfort, and security.

Graham, as cited in Abbey (2011, p.2), writes that *"trusting relationships are demonstrated in various facilitations that require specific interactions between the horse and the participant such as brushing or caring of the horse"*.

Abbey (2011) notes during recurring observation about resilience and coping with trauma, an important healing power is healthy relationships. This powerful positive effect of healthy relational interactions (which include the horse during therapy sessions) on the individual is at the core of relationally based protective mechanisms that help him survive trauma and loss.

Avoiding getting help is often because of the fear of being judged, compartmentalized, and deemed mentally ill. And for the rest, fatalism and cynicism step in and say, "Why bother?" People with untreated trauma sink into the deepest, darkest depth of depression with no apparent way out. They do not dare look up, afraid they might find their ugly trauma looking back down at them. People suffering from trauma are trapped in the past traumatic event. They are frightened of the future because they are afraid the past trauma will be recreated, and live in a fatalistic present. For many, the only relief is from what might become addictive behavior (Milich, 2012).

Used in conjunction with Logotherapy principles, Equine Assisted Therapeutic Facilitation gives participants the capacity for self-regulation, to choose their response and actions and so play an active part in their healing, as well as the ability to consider healthy relationship building, an important element in fostering resilience.

*ST, a 50-year old male, was referred to the facilitation team for anger management by his employer. During ST's journey, the relationship he built with the horses during his weekly sessions often gave him the chance to transfer the lessons he learned and to check his behavior during the week at work. "I had a difference of opinion with my supervisor, but caught myself in time [before he acted in anger] and just walked away. I did not let this go any further – just as the horses would walk away if they did not like something". He explained to the team that he had shared this with his wife that evening, and she had praised him for controlling his temper. At the end of ST's journey, he mentioned how valuable his family was to him, especially his wife's backing and support, during this struggle.*

The horses, by fulfilling the role of catalysts within the metaphorical safe, therapeutic environment, keep the clients in the present; while assisting the clients to re-experience significant life events and relationships, allowing them to work through unresolved conflicts and emotions. They also offer a variety of opportunities for projection and transference, through self-distancing, and, more than often the client can relate to the horses' hypervigilance and impulse to run when feeling frightened of threatened (Klotz et al, 2007). The clients are therefore challenged to change (freedom of will) destructive behavior patterns (creating new neural pathways) and, in the process, forced to focus on their lives in the present (will to meaning) while creating the future (meaning of life). This elicits a wide range of emotions and behaviors in humans, which, in return, acts as catalysts for personal awareness and growth.

*JE, a 30-year old female, after struggling with a severe drug addiction for a number of years, made a decision to attend therapy which she felt would help her to maintain her decision to "remain clean". JE has struggled with self-harming since grade 2 and got involved in drugs during her teens. In the initial therapeutic contacts, JE felt that she had taken a step forward, but over time she began to feel that she was losing control and was on the verge of relapse. JE's journey to find meaning in her life started with her making a conscious decision to take a stand against something (the drugs) that was slowly ruining her life. She had various issues to address, of which several failed relationships were of great importance to her. JE had developed a deeply internalized negative belief system about herself. She saw herself as "being worthless", "not worthy to love" or being loved, as a "disappointment" and "failure". It took intensive sessions working through lots of pain for JE before she was able to discover that she is worthy to receive the good in life. The journey JE is now on portrays the Logotherapy concept of existential vacuum beautifully, her struggle with her will to meaning, and the difficulty to stay in the present while working on creating her future with meaning. Her struggle to overcome her destructive and self-sabotaging behavioral patterns illustrates the need to create new pathways and the difficulty experienced in the process. Her journey, as she is moving ahead, is to realize the impact of the decisions she has made – both past and present, on her current life style and in the future; to take responsibility and be accountable – and this takes huge courage and tenacity and adjusting her attitude to not only life but towards herself is a daily conscious decision on her journey to healing and growth.*

In the facilitation space, the interaction with the horses increases the client's consciousness of his thoughts, words, emotions and actions, thus assisting Logotherapy in its aim to remove the unconscious blocks and bring the human spirit to conscious awareness. Being truthful, congruent, and authentic to ourselves is imperative on the journey to healing. These attributes are enforced during the relational interaction with horses. Letting go of the shackles that hold our minds and spirits captive activates the process of self-transcendence and so completes the healing process.

*IM started therapy with the facilitation team at the age of 18. She lived in Dubai with both her parents from a very young age. She was initially diagnosed with Dyslexia in her first grade and had difficulties adjusting to school. She was involved in several dysfunctional and abusive romantic relationships while at school, which resulted in affecting her school performance and a first suicide attempt around the age of twelve. She suffered some psychotic episodes during this time, which started after she was raped by one of her boyfriends. Although IM was attending traditional psychotherapy, there did not seem to be any sense of breakthrough and it was recommended that a change in therapeutic approach was necessary.*

*The team used the first couple of sessions to explore who IM is, to identify her fears, her nightmares, and her joys. Illustrating her life concretely, the facilitation team used the information and built her world – she had to add the labels (incidences). Looking at how she micro-labeled the individual elements of each of the obstacles was not only fascinating but heart breaking, as the many losses she has experienced in her 18 years surfaced so clearly.*

*Her loss of trust in relationships, her loss of friendships, loss of faith in justice, the loss of her innocence, her loss of accepting herself, of liking herself, of trusting herself, hating herself, and hurting herself and thus her self-worth. So clearly, she showed us all the "messages" she has accumulated over her 18 years that she now believed to be true of herself. During the sessions which followed, the horses profoundly participated during the sessions playing various roles varying from friends to family members to those that had hurt her, and eventually to God who embraced her and loved her – just as she is. The "I am stupid", "I am not worth anything", "I don't like myself", "I am not worth living"; "I am not worth being loved" and "people don't care about me" were but a few of the lies this beautiful child with her sad blue eyes believed. But it was these very messages that made the facilitation team excited, as these were the links to guide IM on her journey discovering with what alternative message she could replace these lies in the safe space of the facilitation space. Finding meaning despite her suffering took IM on a journey where she had to choose to share and to face the past; making the next choice around if and for how long she was willing to hold on and to let the past dictate her future; to then choose to change direction; choose to forgive; and choose to let go and look instead to the future, learning to take the responsibility for her actions and decisions. A journey where fate (childhood incidences) was turned into freedom. A journey leaning daily on the resources nestled in the noetic dimension that, despite everything she had experienced, had remained intact.*

Being in the facilitation space among horses does create slight arousal in the client as there is always an element of unpredictability. It is this state of arousal that creates the metaphorical link to the horses – who instinctively live in this state, and thus, in the facilitation space these two therapeutic modalities beautifully integrate into LT-EAF. It is allowing this process, happening in the present, to evolve during the sessions that elicits discovery and learning.

Discovering themselves, their values, beliefs, strengths and weaknesses – and therefore the meaning in the moment – does not happen while constantly being instructed or taught. The theorist Vygotsky, cited by Gaskill & Perry (2014) mentions that children learn through play, in the process he called scaffolding, often facilitated by a caring and patient adult. Gaskill & Perry (2014) state that play in therapeutic setup appears to be equally effective, regardless of the presenting problem, but cautioned the therapist to be sensitive to the developmental age of the client. Within the modality of Equine Assisted Facilitation, play (often in the form of role play) during a paddock session, has very effectively been used even with adults.

*Learners from an independent preparatory school were experiencing specific or generalized learning difficulties. The aim of the program was to encapsulate and promote each child's strengths, while encouraging them to develop positive coping strategies to overcome their areas of weakness. The topic for the session was the "Friendship Bag". The group consisted of three children, two male (MI and JO) and one female (LO), with varying problems, including Autism, Asperger's, ADHD, and social anxiety. These children struggle with the sense of understanding their own meaning in life and, therefore, the opportunity to begin to learn about making the right choices for themselves, and their impact on those around them, was the challenge. Due to the above, therapy session time was limited to 20 minutes.*

*The "Friendship Bag" was shown to the children and then explained that the content that needed to be added to the bag was hidden in the forest. They, together with their equine partner which they named Jazz, had to go find them (four in total for each bag) and then to return to "base". The facilitators remained at the "base" observing the process. It was interesting to note that they all scattered starting their search. As they progressed, there was an almost natural migration to each other, pooling their resources and helping each other. Arriving back at "base", they presented the objects they found: whistles, pencils and sharpeners, butterfly-shaped crayons, little stress ball faces.*

*The process consisted of careful, simple questions based on the Socratic Dialogue technique, which were posed to the children, and resulted in precious answers during the session. The conclusions reached after some debate, were as follows:*

- *Whistles in the bag will be to blow if there should be any emergency. Exploring what they saw as emergency in friendship, it was concluded if your friends got hurt or were in trouble, and if the trouble was big enough, you would blow the whistle even if your friends ask you not to (keeping dangerous secrets).*

- *Pencils and sharpeners were difficult, and some guidance resulted that they realized we write words on our friends and family every day. Blunt pencils result in hurtful and bad words where sharp pencils are kind words.*

- *Butterfly-shaped crayons (this conclusion astonished the therapists) are like our friendships – they are colorful and fragile, and need to be handled carefully because then they beautifully color pictures.*

- *The faces depicted that each of them was different, yet they were all unique and special.*

*A simple game in nature, producing seriously insightful comments by children generally thought not capable of it. The therapy team trusts that, if they see any of these items during their normal day to day lives, they will remember the "responsibility" of making the "right/ good" choice in looking after their friendships.*

When working with horses, two people can undertake the same task and get completely different results, and this is the beauty of this type of learning. The participants take what they want or need from the experience. Therefore, horses can be great teachers. In this time of complexity and rapid change, it is essential to balance the vast technological resources and multitude of information that is readily available against instinct, self-awareness, and intuition, or our emotional intelligence. Working through horses enables the participant to connect to these often unused, internal resources, and, because it requires out of the box thinking, it is extremely metaphorical and memorable.

*LO, a 25-year old female client, was referred to the facilitation team through the Psychiatric Recovery Institution where she was completing treatment. LO is a twin, but she has always had a very negative relationship with both parents and she has struggled to cope with her over-controlling, wealthy aunt who assumed the financial support for the entire family. LO joined the team and horses and soon it became clear that she had an almost neurotic pursuit to have the controlling power and an unwillingness to let go of it. She was obstructive and uncooperative whenever sessions did not comply with her drive to prove to life that she was in control. Her unwillingness to work with the treatment program resulted in her dismissal from the institution, and thus LT-EAF was terminated.*

*During the same period TE, a 19-year old female, was referred to the facilitation team. She was in her first year at University, and she was battling with relationships. Her concern was that she did not understand what she was continually doing that would cause the breakdown in relationships. TE enthusiastically cooperated with the facilitation team and horses, and as she grew and progressed in self-discovery, she started changing her attitude towards life and the people around her; exercising her freedom to choose her attitude towards circumstances in her life, TE also accepted responsibility and accountability for her decisions, actions and therefore for her life.*

## 8.   The Process in the Facilitation Space

Although there is no prescribed way to start the sessions, within good therapeutic practice, it is important to create an emotional safe space for the client. Explaining the process that will be followed during sessions seems to calm the clients as this modality is not very well known. For those clients with no horse experience, this can be rather threatening. The role of each of the therapists is explained to the client – including why we use horses. The facilitation team is very sensitive to and observant of the non-verbal communication from both the client and the horses. The facilitation team will also, during activities, move away from the client and horse(s) so as not to influence the dynamics happening between them. Checking in/processing will happen during the activities where the client will be encouraged to find their own answers as their journey unfolds.

The examples below depict some typical sessions. It is important to note that these studies have been summarized:

**Case Study 1** (6 sessions)

*PR was referred to us as a shy, 14-year-old girl battling with depression and increased anxiety levels, loss of trust in her own ability as well as in those around her, and being hyper-vigilant. PR's biological mother died when she was four years old. She and her two siblings (aged 18 months and six) were discovered a couple of days after the mother had died, when neighbors reported constant crying of the children. The three girls were later adopted. The older sister NE has multiple psychological problems and has been in and out of psychiatric units, and she has been extremely difficult to control in the family unit, often attacking verbally the other children or the extended family. As a result of this ongoing subversive bullying from NE, PR had to be hospitalized for emotional distress.*

*The therapy team needed to facilitate the process where PR could recognize her anxiety and fear and to discover how to change (attitude) in order to handle herself effectively in the many other situations in which she would find herself.*

*The sessions started off with an exceptionally soft-spoken little girl, scared of horses and hardly able to make eye contact with the facilitation team. Building rapport and winning her trust was the challenge and during this process of finding out who little PR was, she mentioned that she loved reading fantasy stories – and so, in the facilitation space, the fantasy world of PR was created. Each session was built on the previous session and was guided by the need of the client.*

*An obstacle course was built, and a story was created to form the background to the set-up of the sessions to follow:*

*As the strongest and chosen warrior for the king, PR was to slay the dragons stopping the king from finding a very precious heirloom. A trustworthy steed was to accompany her on this journey. The only weapon the king could give PR was that she "may change or do things differently" at any of the obstacles the dragons were protecting, but that she may not remove anything. The rest of her weapons PR would have to collect as she progressed on her journey.*

*PR was then left to go and label the dragons. Sharing with the team, she started at the castle gate and the drawbridge, which was the location of the first two dragons. She labeled Dragon 1 as NE (older sister who scared her) and Dragon 2 as LE (challenging friend at school). She walked to the fork in the road and labeled the obstacle to the left Dragon 3a and the one to the right Dragon 3b, as they were two identical dragons, and named them "Choices". Moving to the cone circle labeled by the team as the Circle of Recovery, PR added the circle as Dragon 4 naming it "Take time and forgive". From there she moved through the zig-zag cones to Dragon 5 which she labeled as "Victory" – a place she had "to give her best shot". PR was then invited to find her steed and start their journey. PR walked up to the chestnut mare, whom she had named Encouragement in a previous session, but Encouragement moved away. PR then approached a grey mare, whom she named Fear in a previous session, who also moved away. A little lost, PR stood still looking around.*

*After some time, the team called "time out" – and PR was asked to share what happened. PR described that she wanted to take Encouragement with her, but "it walked away", she tried Fear and this "also did not work". She then said "I don't know what to do". After some processing, as to the options available to her, she was invited to complete the task. Looking around, PR fetched the halter, walked to Encouragement and asked for help. PR discovered that she had just earned her Weapon 2 – "she may ask for help" – represented by the halter. PR smiled and tried to get Encouragement to move with her – unsuccessfully. Giving PR some time to figure out a way to handle this, she chose to use her newly acquired Weapon 2. Once again there was the opportunity to explore the possibilities and options she had. Changing direction and putting some pressure on the lead, Encouragement started walking and so PR discovered Weapon 3 – "being assertive, yet kind and asking clearly".*

*PR's whole body language changed and she and Encouragement set off through the gates of the castle and over the drawbridge – slaying the first two dragons. At the crossroads, she stood a little while deciding which way she would go. She made her choice and moved to Dragon 3a. She needed to climb into the structure and guide Encouragement around it without knocking it over. Dragon 3a was slain. Checking in with the team, PR shared her experience, which weapons she acquired, and how she used them. Asking her about the crossroads and her decision as to which dragon to tackle first, she made a very interesting comment: "this is like the battle I have choosing between what is expected of me to do and what I should actually do" and she chose to slay "what is expected of me" first.*

*Asking PR if she noticed what weapons the dragons used, she shyly shook her head "No". During processing, using how it played out with the horses when she started the journey, she made the link that Encouragement moved away when she did not believe in herself and did not know what to do. PR concluded that the dragons' weapons were called "causing doubt" and "giving up".*

*The king's search for his heirloom ended in PR joining the team with a big smile on her face. Asking her to share, she explained this journey, that Encouragement nudged her forward, that she battled at the Circle of Recovery, and that, although they knocked over some stuff it was OK as she kept going, giving "it her best shot".*

*Asking PR which of the dragons were the most difficult, she answered "the Circle of Recovery". Asking what about this circle was difficult elicited the answer that "Encouragement made it a bit hard – I had to keep trying a bit harder. I can't just go to the person and say it – I forgive them – it needs time. I need to think about it, even if I don't like it. I cannot just say it if it is not how I feel here (pointing to her heart)". PR was asked if she could share with us how she understands the word "forgiveness". She responded saying "it is when you could say I don't like what you do, but letting it go – not to let it hold you back".*

*This was the end of the king's journey. Our facilitation team was honored to have experienced three more sessions with PR. At her request, therapy was concluded with "Her Journey to Success" – in much the same manner. Encouragement was still there, quietly following her, but Fear became "Awareness" which "helps to protect you". Taking both with her on this last journey, PR became the king's most astute warrior. She changed from an exceptionally shy and anxious girl, to a smiling teen, handling herself at school, standing up for what she thought was right, protecting her friendship circle from those that tried to bully them, and that she can ask for help when she needs it.*

**Case study 2** (3 sessions)

*DA is a young adult male. He is a highly qualified medical professional with a history of drug addiction. He has been admitted to various rehab facilities before the current facilitation team met him. With no other background information available to us, DA was asked to build his world. Two horses were in the facilitation space with him. DA constructed a very tight box with four solid poles resting on four tires. Six lighter poles were criss-crossed on top of the base and the hula hoops placed on top of them. The stack of cones was then placed in the middle underneath all the poles. Sharing with the team, DA explained that this is how his life is looking – constricted and tightly closed – with him in the middle (he saw himself as the cones). With some exploration, DA shared that his life felt like this especially the last five years. While DA was sharing one of the horses walked up to him, standing very close to him. The facilitation team moved away while DA stood stroking the horse – who stood sniffing, nuzzling, interacting with DA around his neck, shoulders and face. The facilitation team checked in with a very emotional DA who then shared that his partner had committed suicide five years ago, by putting up a morphine drip for himself during the night and that he died in the bed next to DA. During the follow up session DA was asked to build "a letter" to his diseased partner, saying all the things he would have like to have said but never got the chance to. What was of great interest to the team was that throughout DA "building" this letter, the same horse that had interacted so closely to him the previous week continued to interact as closely. This time, however, he moved DA away from the "letter" – all the while keeping on touching DA and licking his legs and nibbling at his shoes. Once again DA became very emotional, and named this particular horse his deceased partner, JA. The actions of horse JA were then explored in relation to the feelings of loss and guilt that DA seemed to be experiencing around their relationship, the drugs and his death. DA mentioned that he*

110

*will not run from the responsibility that he introduced JA to drugs, but that perhaps JA is telling him to "let go" – "to move on".*

## 9.  Conclusion

The integrated principles from Gestalt, Reality, Rogerian and Brief therapy found in Equine Assisted Therapeutic Facilitation merge beautifully with the meaning centered therapy principle of Logotherapy, setting the stage for the client to play an active and accountable part in his own healing process. As a therapy where the facilitator may invite and/or confront the client to grow, it is action-orientated with the emphasis on the client's own discovery of answers and inner strengths to deal with challenges. Aligning this with the neurobiological processes, the Logotherapeutic Equine Assisted Therapeutic Facilitation process beautifully borrows from Frankl to maintain that we learn from the past and look to the future with hope – while living in the present. Logotherapeutic Equine Assisted Therapeutic Facilitation creates this space: where the clients can explore their fears, build trust in themselves and others and develop their relational skills in a supportive and non-threatening environment. A process which stretches clients mentally, intellectually, emotionally and spiritually while also enabling the development of new neural networks and finding meaning.

**About the Author**

Marlene du Plessis, BL, Diplomat Clinician Logotherapist, NLP Practitioner – South Africa. Marlene was born and raised in South Africa and is currently in the process of relocating abroad. She is part of a therapeutic team, working closely with a Clinical Psychologist, offering Equine and Nature Assisted facilitation and therapy, focusing particularly on clients with psychiatric diagnosis and/or trauma victims. Becoming the link to self-discovery, and based on Logotherapy principles, both client and therapists listen to the messages conveyed by nature and our horses in a metaphorical safe environment. This process builds a stronger reality for the client, while highlighting where change, growth and development – and so healing – in each client's journey is needed. Clients are enabled to develop healthy relationships with, and perceptions of, themselves and others by being co-responsible for their own healing. Marlene derives a sound understanding and knowledge of human behavior from a holistic approach towards the relationship between human and nature. She holds EAGALA Advance certification, and has completed extensive training in both human and animal interaction, including TIR, Advance Animal Assisted Activity therapy, Animal Behavior (Equine), Natural Lifemanship, Psychology and NLP.

## References


Abbey, B. (2011). *Equine-Assisted Learning: Healing with Horses*. Arabian Horse Reading Literacy Project, pp. 1-3. Retrieved from www.arabianhorsereading.com

Carlsson, C., Ranta, D., & Traeen, B. (2015). Mentalizing and emotional Labor Facilitate Equine Assisted Social Work with Self-harming Adolescents. *Child and Adolescent Social Work Journal*, 329-339.

du Plessis, A. (2016). Dr (Radiologist). (M. du Plessis, Interviewer)

EAGALA. (n.d.). *Fundamentals of EAGALA Model Practice: Training Manual. 7*. EAGALA.

Fine, A. (2010). *Handbook on Animal Assisted Therapy: Theoretical foundations and guidelines for practice* (3 ed.). Elsevier.

Frankl, V. (1963). *Man's Search for Meaning: An Introduction to Logotherapy*. New York: Washington Square Press.

Frankl, V. (1986). *The doctor and the soul: From psychotherapy to logotherapy*. New York: Vintage Books.

Gaskill, R., & Perry, B. (2014). The Neurobiological Power of Play: Using the Neurosequencial Model of Therapeutics to guide Play in the Healing process. *In Creative Arts and Play Therapy for Attachment Problems* (pp. 178-194). New York: Guilford Publications.

Gilgun, J. (2012). *Neurobiology, Trauma, & Child Development*. The NEATS: A Child and Family Assessment, 16.

Kane, B. (2004). Mythology of Horses. Retrieved from Horsensei: http://www.horsensei.com/publications/MythologyofHorses/MythologyOfHorses.pdf

Klontz, B., Bivens, A., Leinart, D., & Klontz, T. (2007). The Effectiveness of Equine-Assisted Experiential Therapy: Results of an Open Clinical Trial. *Society and Animals*, 15, 257-267.

LeDoux, J. (1996). *The Emotional Brain: The Mysterious Underpinnings of Emotional Life*. New York: Touchstone.

Levine, P. (2010). *In an Unspoken Voice: How the Body Releases Trauma and Restores Goodness*. Berkeley, California: North Atlantic Books.

Lobell, J., & Powell, E. (2015, June). Archeology. Retrieved from The Story of the Horse: http://www.archaeology.org/issues/180-features/3345-the-horse-through-history

Love, P. (2016). Universe of Symbolism. Retrieved from Symbolic Meaning of Horse: http://www. universeofsymbolism.com/symbolic-meaning-of-horse.html

Lukas, E. (2000). *Logotherapy Texbook: Meaning-centered Psychotherapy.* (T. Brugger, Trans.) Canada: Liberty Press.

Marshall, M. M. (2012). *Logotherapy Revisited: Review of the Tenets of Viktor E Frankl's Logotherapy.* Ottawa: Ottawa Institute of Logotherapy.

McCormick, A. R., McCormick, M., & McCormick, T. (2004). *Horses and the Mystical Path: The Celtic Way of Expanding the Human Soul.* Novato: New World Library.

Meyer, W., Moore, C., & Viljoen, H. (2008). *Personology: From Individual to Ecosystem* (4 ed.). Johannesburg: Heinemann Publishers (Pty)Ltd.

Milich, N. (2012). Your Brain and Trauma. Retrieved from Psychology Today: https://www. psychologytoday.com/blog/the-time-cure/201211/your-brain-trauma

Odendaal, J. (2002). *Pets and our Mental Health.* Vantage Press, Inc.

Perry, B. (2004, September). Maltreatment and the Developing Child: How Early Childhood Experience Shapes Child and Culture. The Margaret McCain Lecture Series. Centre for Children & Families in the Justice System.

Perry, B., & Hambrick, E. (2008). The Neurosequential Model of Therapeutics. *Reclaiming children and youth,* 17(3), pp. 38-43.

Rossouw, P. (2013). The neuroscience of talking therapies. Implications for therapeutic practice. ResearchGate. Retrieved 2016, from https://www.researchgate.net/publication/257811205_ The_neuroscience_of_talking_therapies_Implications_for_therapeutic_ practice?enrichId=rgreq-0a886624e595f522c20f00659546d3cb-XXX&enrichSource =Y292ZXJQYWdlOzI1NzgxMTIwNTtBUzo5NzA0MjU1ODg4MTgw NEAxNDAwMTQ4MTU

Shantell, T. (2002). *Life's Meaning in the Face of Suffering. Jerusalem*: The Hebrew University Magnes Press.

Sutton, L. (2015). *Animal-Assisted Logotherapy: An Exploration of the Human-Animal Bond.* Victor Frankl Institute of Ireland.

Trotter, K. (2012). *Harnessing the Power of Equine Assisted Counceling: Adding Animal Assisted Therapy to your practise.* New York: Routledge.

Wach, S. (2014). *Horses, Mindfulness and Psychiological Response.* Psychology Department: University of South Carolina Scholar Commons.

Weiten, W. (2015). *Psychology. Themes and Variations* (2de South African Edition ed.). (J. Hassim, Ed.) Cengage Learning, Marinda Louw.

Wikipedia. (2016). Play Therapy. Retrieved from Wikipedia: https://en.wikipedia.org/wiki/ Play_therapy

Wilson, R. (2014). *Neuroscience for Councellors.* London: Jessica Kingsley Publishers.

Wong, P. (2012). From Logotherapy to Meaning-Centered Counseling and Therapy. In P. Wong, *The Human Quest for Meaning: Theories, Research and Applications* (2 ed., pp. 619-647). Taylor and Francis Group, LLC.

Wong, P. (2014). Viktor Frankl's meaning seeking model and positive psychology. In A. Batthyani, & P. Russo-Netzer, *Meaning in existential and positive psychology.* New York: Springer.

Wylie, M. (n.d). *The Limits of Talk: Bessel van der Kolk wants to transform the treatment of trauma.* Psychotherapy Networker.

CHAPTER 22

# Horses as Sentient Beings in Psychodynamic Equine Assisted Trauma Therapy (pEATT)

Ilka Parent

*Since 2007, psychodynamic Equine Assisted Trauma Therapy (pEATT) has developed primarily from the needs of the practice in Equine Assisted Psychotherapy for clients suffering from traumatic events. PEATT is an integrative approach: it combines proven trauma-therapeutic techniques taken from Ego State Therapy, Schema Therapy and Psychodynamic Imaginative Trauma-therapy while providing the psychodynamic framework. Horses are considered sentient members of the team providing this type of therapy. PEATT has evolved as an approach for treating complex Posttraumatic Stress Disorder (PTSD) and is being researched in treating combat related complex PTSD. It fulfills the demands for a trauma-adapted treatment within proven psychotherapeutic procedures.*

The psychiatric disorder commonly known as Post-traumatic Stress Disorder (PTSD) is associated with serious consequences that may lead to poor quality of life and many comorbid occurrences. Traumatic experiences can have significant effects, impacting brain functioning and resulting in neurological, physiological, and psychological changes. Cognitive processes, including memory storage and verbalization skills, change. (Van der Kolk & McFarlane, 2012). Trauma often takes place in a toxic relational context. The traumatic event sets ways of coping and interacting in ongoing relationships that frequently become a pattern. Dysfunctional, self-regulatory mechanisms are established – all of which, in turn, inhibit future trust in people and potential caregivers. Even if trauma has been processed cognitively, dysfunctional relationship patterns are often still in place.

To effectively treat relational trauma, treatment needs to take place in a relational context. Current trauma therapeutic approaches[1] focus on enhancing the abilities to self-regulate and self-accept while re-processing the traumatic event(s). The traditional domain of psychodynamic theories[2], which emphasize a trusting and secure therapeutic relationship, is particularly appealing. In addition to utilizing the therapeutic relationship, pEATT values an empathetic self-acceptance and integrates frequent interactions with horses in the treatment process. In addition to specific trauma confrontative activities[3], engaging in activities with horses allows clients to restore a sense of self-awareness, and, in true psychodynamic tradition, insight into their present. Several processes take place simultaneously:

- Clients are given the opportunity to establish a relationship with another non-human being. When there is a history of relational trauma, animals are often perceived as less threatening than humans. Horses have been part of mankind's history for more than 5000 years, and are often regarded as gentle and powerful beings. Many times, there is a natural curiosity to engage with these animals. Horses themselves are curious as well, and they take an interest in any human entering their space. As social beings, they will interact with humans if these are not perceived as threatening. Horses are authentic and true to their nature in their interactions. They do not have a human agenda or preconceived human notions about unknown people entering their space. As clients are invited to work through structured activities in the presence of the horses, relational dynamics between horses and humans occur and develop. When attempting to form a relationship, the client's dysfunctional behavioral and relational patterns come out: because even after trauma has been processed cognitively, old, non-functioning relationship patterns are often still in place. Therefore, clients naturally repeat their acquired relationship

---

1 Common activities include derivatives from exposure, reprocessing, such as EMDR, and somatic theories.

2 The goal of "psychodynamic" trauma therapy is to identify which phase of the traumatic response the individual is stuck in. Once this is discerned, the therapist can determine which aspects of the traumatic event interfere with the processing and integration of the trauma. Common elements of psychodynamic therapy include taking the individual's developmental history and childhood into account, placing emphasis on understanding the meaning of the trauma and looking at how the trauma has impacted the individual's sense of self and relationships, as well as what has been lost due to the traumatic event.

3 Equine assisted traumaconfrontative activities in pEATT may include concepts and interventions introduced by the Ego State Therapy, Schema Therapy and Psychodynamic Imaginative Traumatherapy, and at times include derivatives of the standardized EMDR protocoll. All of these serve to specifically address and reprocess certain traumatic events while either being in the presence of horses or on horse back.

patterns when attempting to form a relationship with a horse. The horses, in turn, react and respond true to their nature to these behaviors, often showing behaviors clients typically only experience from other human beings. As horses are often perceived as less threatening than humans, it is easier for clients to identify the horses' behaviors as patterns that may be reactions to their own behaviors. Consequently, clients can recognize their dysfunctional contributions when attempting to build relationships. A transfer from what is being experienced with the horses to the human realm is then possible.

- As clients work through their topics while engaging in interactions with horses, they are invited to place their projections onto the horses. Therapists can thus obtain information about underlying thoughts, feelings and unconscious processes through the clients' projections onto and the identifications with the horses. Throughout the millennia, humans have seen various abilities in horses and have attributed various characteristics to them[4]. During the processing, the therapist listens to the conflicts and the topics expressed by the client in his answers to the equine specialist's questions. He listens for the metaphors the client uses and pays attention to symbols that were employed during the human-horse interaction. In contrast to traditional talk therapy, clients are not confronted with interpretations but with the horses' reactions to their behavior. In a way, the horses' reactions have two functions: on the one side, they are a massive projection screen for the client, and, on the other side, an amplifying glass for the treatment team.

- During sessions, clients are asked to set up and build their internal representations with real objects. Due to the effects of trauma on cognitive abilities, clients who have suffered from a traumatic event often struggle with abstract concepts and are not always able to put some of their experiences into words. By using objects as symbols to create and build a representation of their internal images, a stage representative of their inner world is created. Asking clients to label their items enables them to identify their internal world and allows for self-distancing. Labeling also emotionally charges them. Horses typically detect and respond to non-verbal communication cues differently

---

4   The human's tendency to attribute human traits, emotions, and intentions to animals or non-human entities is called anthropomorphism. In pEATT, this natural tendency to speak for animals is used and so-called projections on the horses are noted and collected.

and arguably more sensitively than humans. It is the horses' actions and reactions to the clients and their objects that are being observed and noted by the treating team. During processing, these observations are given back to the clients in a structured questioning format, allowing for clients to reflect upon, gain insights and distance themselves from their internal images and another being's responses to their nonverbal cues.

In short, in pEATT, clients experience interactions with horses on a stage that represents their real life and facilitates an insight into their everyday behaviors that they may not be able otherwise to verbalize or be conscious of previously.

## Horses as Sentient Beings in the Treatment Team

In pEATT, horses are seen as equal team members. Participating horses are not objectified, they are no tools. They are seen as sentient beings, with the same rights as their human counterparts.

These three sentences summarize one of pEATT's core principles. If you do not feel comfortable doing what you are asking your horse to do yourself, or feel comfortable asking your human team mate to do, then the horses should not be asked to do it.

PEATT provides a detailed "job description" for all of its team members, including the horses. When working according to the pEATT guidelines, horses are not to be instrumentalized, meaning they do not serve a function, nor a purpose, nor are they the means to or an agent for change any more than their human counterpart. As stated before, it is instrumental when working with relational trauma that treatment takes place in a relational context, and part of the approach is providing clients the opportunity to establish a relationship – initially with horses. One may justifiably ask if putting horses with people in a restricted space disregards their inherent right to choose, and does not consider their well-being. However, in pEATT, establishing a relationship with the horses is never part of the treatment goal. If it occurs, it does so as a side effect. PEATT focuses on the internal representations clients bring with them, and treatment is set up to process past trauma, while enhancing a person's ability to experience life in the here and now. Even if the horses are not engaging with the client, correlating relational skills can still be processed. This is an essential difference to some other approaches in that it maintains its ethical concept of not forcing another being to do anything but what one chooses for oneself.

To facilitate this core principle, horses are given as much room as possible when taken to work with clients: most work is being done on pastures that are at least the size and diameter of a dressage riding arena, if not at least one acre. The number of horses is dependent on the space available. Horses are never used alone, preferably in threes. Horses are assessed prior to sessions as to their willingness to work. It has been my experience that we have had horses literally dragging us to the arena instead of their pasture when the decision was made not to have them work that day. We have also had horses who clearly indicated that they did not want to be in the same space as clients. At times, we have had horses jump fences to be with clients instead of "free of work" and vice versa. Ultimately, it is up to the horses to "be a horse", and to have free choice whether they want to interact with humans or not. If the horses do not wish to engage, they are not asked or forced to do so. Clients are not taught or lectured about horse training techniques or horse specifics. The use of restrictive training aids, such as halters and lead ropes, is typically not part of pEATT. A tied down horse no longer has the ability to avoid a tight situation. There is no objective for the horses to meet, and there is no right or wrong way for the horses to act. In all equine assisted work, horses are able to act and react according to their needs and their nature. Under ideal conditions, during the session horses can simply act and react to their environment, including clients' nonverbal communication signals. In pEATT, horses are not regarded as therapists or more knowledgeable than psychotherapists. They are seen as sentient beings with individualized needs, wants, and desires, who possess a different form of perception inherent in their species. Much controversy exists pertaining to interpreting horses metaphorically, and, as a consequence, horses suffering from the emotional burden associated with these metaphors. The work with client-generated metaphors is an integral part of pEATT. The key term is "client-generated metaphors": metaphors are never imposed on the horses by the treatment team, no more than metaphors are imposed on the human team members. When metaphors are client generated, they are projections and part of the forming relationship that may or may not be developing – and the horse retains the choice to leave the interaction at any given time. In pEATT, at times, clients are placed on top of horses, to be carried by them – or horses are led on a leadline by both client and equine specialist. These activities, as seldom as they occur, are specific tools to assist in trauma confrontations utilizing derivatives of the standard EMDR protocol. During such activities, the horses' choice is limited. Much care and thought has been given to consider the horses' well-being under such circumstances. Having an equine specialist on the team who is knowledgeable about horses in general, and their mental well-being in particular, is one of the standards that pEATT maintains. All horses that carry clients on their backs are used to being ridden outside of their therapeutic work. The Equine Specialist has to be certified as a therapeutic riding instructor. Above all, the horses' reactions are observed and considered; if the horse does not want to participate, it is never forced to engage in the activity, but instead its reaction is processed with the client. Typically, it is those situations where the horses "do not cooperate" that serve the greatest therapeutic value, as the horse's reactions reflect some internal struggles of which neither the client nor the human treatment team members may be aware. In summary, one can conclude that, despite their belonging to a different species, horses are seen as valuable team members with no more or less areas of responsibility and rights than their human counterparts. The team approach entails four experts: one for human and clinical issues (psychotherapist), one for horses (equine specialist), one for perceiving non-verbal cues and reactions (horses), and one for coming up with insights and solutions (client).

## About the Author

Ilka B. Parent, Dipl.-Psych., Clinical Psychologist (TP), Traumatherapist (DeGPT). Years of experience of working in military hospitals and in private practice schooled her in the clinical areas concerning military service members. Her clinical focus on issues typically associated with serving in the Armed Forces had to adjust after 9/11 to the areas of "Trauma", "Combat Related Stress Disorders" and "Reintegration" after deployments or retirement. To date, she offers military service members and their families as well as people who have experienced trauma assistance in dealing with their respective life circumstances.

## References

Parent, I.B. (2016). Fundamentals of Equine Assisted Trauma Therapy. CreateSpace Independent Publishing Platform.

CHAPTER 23

# Somatic Experiencing® and Attachment Principles

## Increasing Safety and Welfare in Equine-Assisted Interventions and Horsemanship Approaches

Sarah Schlote

*Equine-Facilitated Trauma Therapy is an integrative approach to trauma treatment for humans, which integrates principles of trauma-informed care with attachment theory, ego state work (Schlote & Parent, 2018, in press), and touch work, along with theory and practices from Somatic Experiencing® (the latter being referred to as EQUUSOMA).*

The principles upon which this approach are founded have useful applications not only for the field of equine-assisted interventions but also horsemanship and training methods. In particular, Somatic Experiencing® is a psychophysiological approach to healing from trauma and chronic stress, based on mammalian stress physiology and other interdisciplinary fields of study. Developed by Dr. Peter A. Levine in the 1960s, it is based on the foundational premise that wild animals, though routinely facing threats, rarely exhibit signs of trauma. Although wild animals have the ability to naturally "discharge" the build-up of thwarted survival energy following the freeze/immobility response, domesticated or captive animals often do not, as a result of being restrained or prevented in some way from completing specific defensive actions or from acting on their natural drives for movement, exploring the environment, foraging, and social engagement (safety, bonding, soothing, play). When animals experience fear or are frightened when going into freeze, it takes longer for them to come out of tonic immobility (a time-limited experience that is usually characterized by self-paced termination), or collapse (learned helplessness, defeat, shut down, submission).

Humans are in a similar boat as domesticated animals. Living in a "social cage", humans typically neo-cortically override the body's natural impulses or discharge/release through rationalization, fear, self-judgment, enculturation, and shame. Whether due to physical, emotional, or mental restraint, the outcome is similar: organic self-regulation is disrupted and the system does not re-set. As stated by Levine (1997), *this residual energy does not simply go away. It persists in the body, and often forces the formation of a wide variety of symptoms, e.g., anxiety, depression, and psychosomatic and behavioral problems. These symptoms are the organism's way of containing (or controlling) the undischarged residual energy*" (p. 20). Levine proposes the concept of renegotiation as crucial to recovery from chronic stress and trauma. This idea of renegotiation is a foundational principle that can guide equine-based programs and horsemanship in a trauma-informed way. He states:

*Renegotiation is not about simply reliving a traumatic experience. It is, rather, the gradual and titrated revisiting of various sensory-motor elements comprising a particular trauma. Renegotiation occurs primarily by accessing procedural memories associated with the two dysregulated states of the autonomic nervous system (hyper/hypo-arousal) and then restoring and completing the associated active responses. As this progresses, the client moves towards equilibrium, relaxed alertness, and here-and-now orientation.* (Levine, 2015, p. 44)

Renegotiation is different from re-enactment. It supports a different outcome to a familiar situation or dilemma, experiencing oneself differently in a familiar circumstance, and experiencing relationships differently. When we "feel felt" by the other, when there is responsiveness and attunement to emotional, somatic, and relational cues, and when we are supported to take effective action in the moment based on our needs and what is wanting to happen, "corrective emotional experiences" (i.e., "corrective somatic experiences") are possible. This is quite different from having choice taken away, being silenced without a voice, having to override and shutdown in order to be in relationship, or having to block one's natural impulses towards safety and self-protection. As discussed by Schlote[1] (2017), a trauma lens and trauma-informed care principles of safety, consent, choice, voice, empowerment, trust, collaboration and compassion apply as much to the humans in the intervention or the horsemanship approach as the animals. Within the context of Somatic Experiencing® as an intervention,

*Individuals locked in anxiety or rage then relax into a growing sense of peace and safety. Those stuck in depression gradually find their feelings of hopelessness and numbness transformed into empowerment, triumph, and mastery. SE trauma resolution catalyzes corrective bodily experiences that contradict those of fear and helplessness. This resets the nervous system, restores inner balance, enhances resilience to stress, and increases people's vitality, equanimity, and capacity to actively engage in life* (Somatic Experiencing® Trauma Institute).

A similar outcome is possible for the horses as well when related to from this perspective – greater aliveness, regulation, connection and agency as opposed to living in their survival brain as a baseline state. And, ideally, in horse-human relationships there will be a sense of reciprocity and secure attachment as opposed to one member of the relationship having all the control. This requires the ability to attend to what is occurring in the relationship and what is happening in the nervous systems of both horse and human.

## 1. The Activation Cycle Map

A number of authors have proposed that self-protective responses occur in a hierarchical sequence. This sequence is known by different names depending on the source, such as the activation cycle or defense response cycle (Foundation for Human Enrichment, 2007), the preparatory set (Payne & Crane-Godreau, 2015), and the defense cascade (Kozlowska et al., 2015). Schlote (2018, in press) describes the process as follows:

*When faced with novelty in the environment, our first response is to arrest/startle and orient to the source of the stimulation. Herd mammals turn to group members to confirm or disconfirm whether or not there is danger, and also rely on one another for survival efforts*

---

1  See Chapter 15 in volume 1.

*and safety. If a threat is identified, both horses and humans will engage in specific defensive actions (fight/flight), or freeze (immobilize) or submit if these are not successful or possible. This appraisal of safety or threat and hierarchy of responses occurs in rapid succession, often beyond conscious awareness, and rarely results in trauma in wild animals. The main difference between domesticated species and our wild cousins is that they are generally not exposed to the same long-term stressors as humans and domesticated animals are. They are also typically free to engage in natural behaviour and protective actions, and move through the immobility response by shaking and discharging whatever thwarted survival energy is left in the system to return to a state of balance.*

Aside from orienting and the standard canon of fight, flight, freeze, fold, and faint[2], mammals also have an additional defense response strategy: fawn. According to Dr. Stephen Porges, creator of the polyvagal theory, social engagement is the primary strategy by which mammals ensure survival that distinguishes us from reptiles and other earlier organisms. Bonding, affiliative behaviors and secure attachment relationships are sources of safety as well as the foundation for healthy development. Social strategies can arise as defensive responses as well, whether before progressing to fighting or fleeing, or when it is clear that fight or flight is not possible. These include the attachment cry, clinging to caregivers, and tending and befriending behavior such as caretaking, appeasing, pleasing, and so on. Furthermore, the freeze response not only occurs when fight or flight are not possible, but also when social engagement strategies are not possible or do not feel safe (such as turning away from social contact as a survival response, like distancing, withdrawing, and shutting down, as opposed to turning towards social contact). Some have proposed other "Fs" as well, including fidget, fright, and fornicate. Fidget does not constitute a defensive response per se, but is rather a displacement behavior showing evidence of early fight or flight activation at the lower end of the activation cycle (such as when feeling nervous, uncomfortable or irritable), or of thwarted or uncompleted fight or flight energy (such as jittery legs or hands when highly charged but unable to leave or fight back in a particular situation). Fidget might

---

2   Faint, mostly commonly caused by vasovagal syncope, is not known to exist in other animals aside from humans. The reasons for this are currently unknown (Blanc, Alboni & Benditt, 2015).

also, at times, refer to self-stimulating activities when facing distress or shutdown (a form of management or coping strategy), or be evidence of both. In either case, fidget is not included in the activation cycle graph above but is nonetheless an observable action that, along with other stereotypical behavior (Schlote, 2017) can provide information about nervous system arousal or activation. Fright (referring to immobility states) is typically used to denote the freeze response by authors who instead use the word freeze to describe the startle/arrest response that occurs when first noticing novelty in the environment (Blanc, Alboni & Benditt, 2015; Kozlowska et al., 2015). In keeping with that particular language usage, then freeze would show up where startle/arrest is on the activation cycle graph, and the word freeze currently at the apex of the bell curve would be replaced with fright for an equivalent effect. Finally, although the function of sex is not primarily to be self-protective, fornicate could be considered a sub-category under "fawn", a form of social engagement strategy in the face of perceived danger in certain circumstances. As such, it too does not have its own denotation in the diagram below but is an example that falls within the model nonetheless.

*Figure 1: The Activation Cycle*

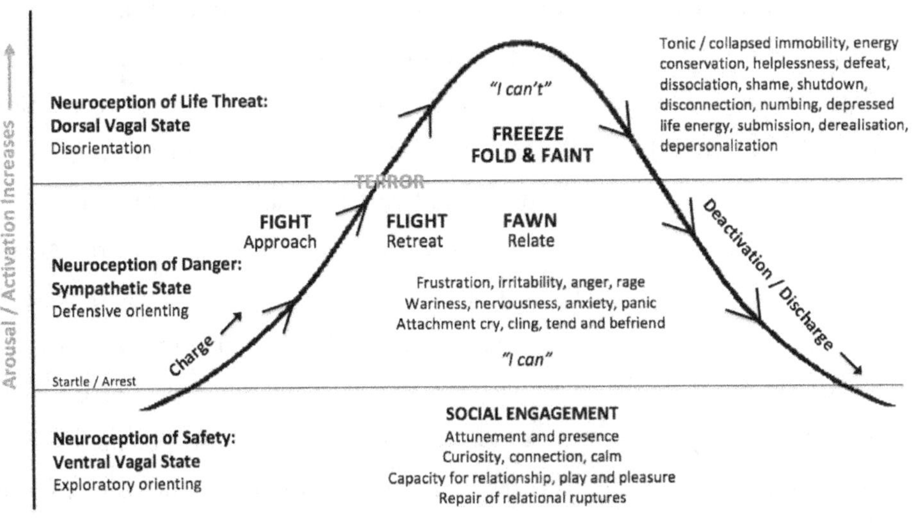

The activation cycle corresponds somewhat to the idea of working with the window of tolerance, a concept created by Dr. Daniel Siegel (1999), which is the better known of the two maps. The window of tolerance model provides a useful visual representation of hyper- and hypo-arousal and the range between the two extremes. For some, the range is narrower, while for others it is wider. The activation cycle, on the other hand, depicts the hierarchical progression in the defense cascade, and conveys the "as they go in, so they come out" quality of the freeze response. As such, the defense response activation cycle provides a helpful map for gauging where both equines and humans are in the context of equine-assisted interventions (and, indeed, with regards to other human-animal interactions, like when training or competing in various disciplines). Being able to tell if a particular activity is within a tolerable range, at the edge where growth occurs, or if it is taking a person or animal beyond their capacity or threshold, sending them into survival physiology, is important in order to ensure that equine-assisted interventions and horsemanship activities are mutually beneficial and that the wellness or safety or growth of one does not come at the expense of the other. This is not always easy to do, of course. For instance, a state of quiet or stillness can be misleading, and there are subtle physiological, behavioral and relational cues that indicate when it is indicative of being calm and connected, bored and tuned out, dissociated and disconnected, suppressing or masking emotion (more exclusively a human behavior, often due to shame), or shutdown and compliant. Important information about a horse's or human's state can be missed if we are not paying attention to the nuances of the somatic experience as it arises moment by moment in the course of relationship. For instance, Hunter (2017) describes her experience of misinterpreting stillness as cooperation when in fact her horse was in a freeze state and merely compliant due to pain from a large insect that had burrowed its way into the horse's sheath. Missing out on these cues can result in situations that do not feel good for either member in the dynamic – in terms of the pain the horse was overriding to go along with his human's request, the pain or injury the human might have endured when the horse thawed out of freeze into reactivity in response to being bitten (had the horse bucked in reaction to the discomfort), and the overall experience of misattunement and not being seen or heard accurately by the other.

*Becoming attuned to the difference between compliance, which comes from the survival part of the brain, and cooperation, which comes from the "thinking" part of the brain, begins with noticing the contrast between an individual who is frozen vs. one who is consciously choosing to cooperate with a request. Rather than being attuned when Partner got very still, I became task-oriented thinking it was great that things were going so smoothly. And yet he was hurting inside the entire time… if I had just noticed that his eyes were a bit vacant, or his breathing a bit shallow, I might have continued exploring whether that fly had really gone away. Sometimes we have to stop and consider whether we are really attuned to the other and accurately interpreting their signals in order to build and deepen our relationship* (Hunter, 2017).

This example shows how a thwarted self-protective response in the activation cycle might become a safety concern in a horse-human interaction. If an animal is prevented from completing a particular impulse (especially towards survival or self-protection – trying to swat at the fly) by shutting down to comply with the human, there can be potential risks for both individuals. For instance, there are programs that require horses to always be tied on a lead line, with no ability to escape or choose to move away when feeling uncomfortable. The prevailing belief within some of these programs is that the horses must be on a line to ensure safety for the human participants, and that horses must be under control at all times, meaning activities that take place at liberty are considered to be at increased risk. However, the opposite is often true. By preventing the animal's natural ability to move away or create distance in relationship, especially when feeling uncomfortable or scared, a build-up of frustrated or thwarted fight or flight response energy under the shutdown of compliance could lead to explosive responses that place humans and horses further at risk when the horses eventually thaw out of the frozen submission into aliveness and begin voicing their opinions.

Similarly, stress arousal does not mean that an animal (or human) is in survival activation. While all activation involves arousal, not all arousal is considered activation. Indeed, beyond pain, confusion and distress, one can experience stress arousal in the sympathetic nervous system that is either pleasant or enjoyable (such as excitement, anticipation of something desired, play or sex, aliveness, and so on), or unpleasant but not intolerable (such as getting an injection, building confidence around objects that seem unfamiliar or spooky, etc.). Energy can be misleading, and it too requires an ability to notice subtle cues that would help determine if it constitutes arousal or hyper-arousal, stress or distress, vigilance or hyper-vigilance, and so on. There are also individual differences to consider – what might be tolerable arousal for one might be activating for another. It is important to take each organism's history, personality, species, needs, nervous system, and capacity for social engagement into account when facilitating equine-assisted interventions, and attune to the nuanced ways the personality and nervous system express themselves emotionally, cognitively and somatically moment by moment.

Another reason why it can be difficult to ensure that the horse-human relationship does not rely on one member of the relationship benefiting at the expense of the other is that a number of horsemanship methods tend to promote either end of the continuum of reciprocity as opposed to the center. For instance, many horsemanship models continue to promote dominance and control of the horse, under the guise of "leadership" or using gentler methods, where the human is in charge (as seen with certain natural horsemanship methods), while other models promote a view where the horse has all the choice and control (such as certain liberty training approaches). When the relationship is entirely on the human's terms or entirely on the horse's terms, at least one member of the relationship's needs are not getting met, which results in an imbalance in the relationship dynamic. As stated by Jobe and Shultz-Jobe (2016), "if it is not a good principle for building healthy relationships with people, then we do not use it with horses, and vice versa" (p. 32). Indeed, if being in relationship requires one member of the relationship to not have choice or a voice, feel deprived, or have to resort to survival strategies (fight, flight, fawn or freeze) in order to be with the other member, then this is not a sign of a healthy, secure relationship. In human-to-human relationships and human therapy, this would be a given, yet somehow this seems like a radical idea when building relationships with horses or in horsemanship, where the things are typically one sided and physical and psychological control (viewed as abuse in human relationships) are more common. Although there continues to be a prevailing opinion that being safe around horses requires the human to be in control, bringing in the understanding of the activation cycle and progression from safety in connected relationships, to danger (fight, flight, fawn responses), to life threat (freeze, fold, faint) helps provide a much more nuanced map from which to gauge the horse-human relationship.

## 2.   Fostering Safety Via Titration

An understanding of the activation cycle map does not imply that it is advisable to avoid higher states of arousal or activation altogether. However, it does mean that working more gradually to build capacity in the nervous system is recommended before progressing to higher thresholds, whether pleasant or unpleasant, in order to be able to experience them without dissociating, shutting down, overriding or engaging in other defensive accommodations to manage. Doing activities that involve higher degrees of connection (proximity, touch, attunement) or the mobilization of greater intensity (such as with boundary setting exercises or approaching something that is anxiety- or fear-inducing) can bring both horse and human closer to the "trauma vortex" (Levine, 1997), where there is a greater amount of bound activation coupled into horse-human experiences that could be uncomfortable but helpful, or might even be considered life-enhancing (such as being approached, intimacy, relationship, separation, assertiveness, joy and even calm being over-coupled with fear or shame). The closer to the centre of the "vortex", the more dysregulation and the more survival responses (hypervigilance, fighting/resistance, fleeing/avoidance, fawning/appeasement/clinging, or freezing) or management strategies[3] kick in to cope (like addictions, stereotypies, shame, and so on). Proceeding with caution and curiosity is important and involves two concepts taught in Somatic Experiencing®: titration and pendulation. Titration refers to the idea of working with smaller amounts of stimulation before proceeding to larger amounts, including the related concept of working at the periphery before

---

3   This does not mean that management strategies are evidence that an organism is always beyond threshold. Some strategies become habit and occur even at lower thresholds of stimulation or activation, having been potentially useful in the past at higher levels and now a familiar and automatic strategy.

moving to the core (or center of the "vortex"). Pendulation refers to the organism's natural ebb and flow between arousal and settling, activation and deactivation, charge and discharge. The activation cycle, if seen through to deactivation and settling, aliveness, and reconnection with others, would constitute a complete pendulation. Being able to tolerate smaller titrations of a particular stimulus and sitting through pendulations of arousal and settling at lower thresholds helps build capacity to experience activities or interactions at progressively higher thresholds (see Figure 2). It is by experiencing the completion of incrementally larger pendulations that the window of tolerance grows and supports resilience when opening up to more of what life has to offer, whether positive or negative. The degree of attention given to the threshold of the activity or request, and the degree of attunement to the organism's capacity to sit through the associated activation and deactivation of the stress response, help reduce the likelihood of flooding, overriding, dissociation or shutdown (through excessive stimulation or pushing for more than is possible at the moment) as well as avoidance (no stimulation provides nothing to work with). Finding that edge between too much and not enough is where the growth and renegotiation occurs.

For instance, an activity involving leading a horse could involve a number of smaller steps that could be worked through first before actual leading – in fact, the goal of leading may be secondary to working on the negotiation of activation and relationship leading up to it. Tracking and working through anticipation activation (pre-emptive charge present in the body) related to simply the idea of approaching and leading a horse is worth exploring first before beginning, then inviting the clients to notice what is happening in their bodies as they approach along with noticing the response of the horse to being approached (non-verbal signs of aversion/no, attraction/yes, maybe or other signs of where the animal might be at on the activation cycle). Taking the time to map out and track through nervous system responses can provide a different experience for both client and horse – a renegotiation as opposed to an unconscious and emotionally unsafe re-enactment of past experiences where both may have had to override or comply to be in relationship. Paying attention to the subtlety of non-verbal cues when approaching one another in the "dance of relationship" is not only promoted within

Somatic Experiencing® and attachment-oriented models of human trauma therapy (Kain & Terrell, 2016), but also in certain horsemanship approaches. One example is what is taught in certain liberty training models, where building relationship at liberty starts at a distance, noticing one's own emotions and noticing horse body language, approaching when detecting signs of consent and stepping back and pausing when noticing activation or signs of aversion, waiting for non-verbal cues within oneself and externally in the horse that it is safe to proceed with approaching and, eventually, creating contact (Resnick, 2005; Wright, 2017). This idea of approaching one another recognizing thresholds or boundaries is consistent with the principles of titration and pendulation and similar to boundaries exercises as taught in Somatic Experiencing®. One important consideration, however, will be ensuring that the dance of relationship at liberty does not solely favor the horse's needs and includes the human's needs as well so that both are finding fulfillment in the relationship (Jobe & Shultz-Jobe, 2016).

*Figure 2: Titration and Thresholds of Intensity*

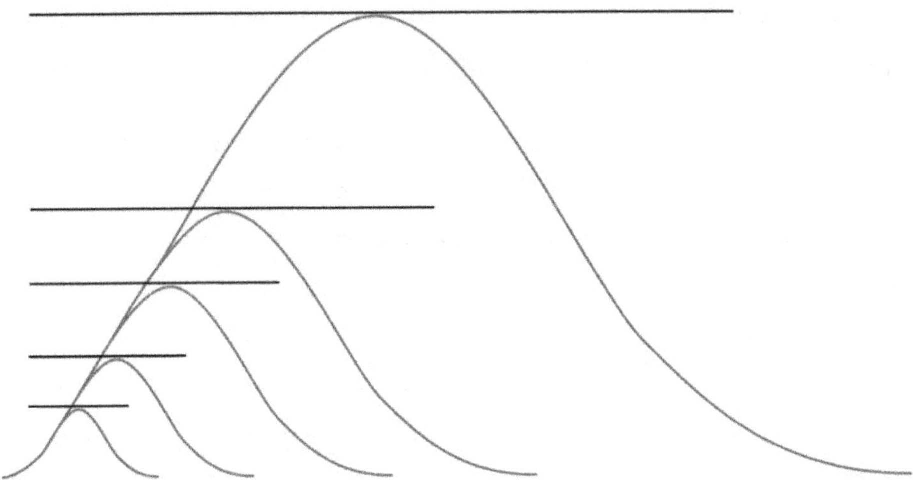

Another example consists of boundary setting exercises where humans may have to increase their energy in order to communicate a boundary effectively with a horse that is less respectful of personal space. For some, raising their energy and mobilizing assertive movement in their limbs can be over-coupled with a lot of unresolved, bound activation (fear, shame, flashbacks to times they were punished or harmed for defending or asserting themselves, etc.). Being able to titrate at smaller thresholds (such as tracking through the activation related to imagining raising one's arms), then working with smaller segments of the movement sequence that would lead to eventually being able to raise one's arms with more intensity with confidence, would also be an example of a renegotiation leading to both greater safety and clearer boundaries in the world, in relationships and with the horses. This is similar but different to the idea of exposure therapies with horses and humans; while both feature a graduated approach, the focus is not on deconditioning of a response to desensitize, but rather on building capacity to work through whatever unresolved charge is left, resulting in changes at a neural level in the nervous system's response patterning. Although the following description by Payne, Levine and Crane-Godreau (2015) focuses specifically on trauma memory work in humans, the description may potentially also have relevance to doing anything that approaches the "trauma vortex" or connects with unresolved activation overall:

*Somatic Experiencing specifically avoids direct and intense evocation of traumatic memories, instead approaching the charged memories indirectly and very gradually, as well as facilitating the generation of new corrective interoceptive experiences that physically contradict those of overwhelm and helplessness. [...] Fear conditioning extinction is the canonical model for recovery from PTSD, especially through exposure therapy; however conditioning theory states that, in the extinction process, a conditioned fear response is not actually eradicated but only suppressed by competing (positive) conditioned experiences. The implication of this, born out by experience, is that, although fear de-conditioning is quick and effective, it is also easily disrupted, as re-exposure to trauma-related cues easily reinstate the fear response. By contrast, clinical experience in SE demonstrates a very robust change in fear responses which are remarkably resistant to re-evocation; this is consistent with the theory that clinical changes mediated by the SE process are not primarily due to fear conditioning extinction but to a discontinuous alteration in core response network dynamical functioning. [...] This going back and forth between charge/activation and discharge/deactivation needs to be finely tuned. Too much of one or the other, and the process of re-establishing balanced functioning is interrupted. This distinguishes SE from exposure therapies, which do not tend to avoid extremes of activation. SE terms this back and forth process "pendulation". When skilfully nurtured it tends to occur spontaneously as the system seeks to restore balance [pp. 1, 6, 7, 8].*

This brings a new perspective to exposure-based approaches, not only with humans with trauma but also in working with horses in terms of horsemanship training, the goal being to build capacity in the nervous system as opposed to simply tune out and tolerate. Horses and humans who learn to simply shut down or numb out in the face of certain stimuli (such as facing feared objects or situations) are likely to be re-activated again in the future into the same response again when they experience enough stimulation that wakes them up out of freeze or dissociation. Tracking the activation cycle and paying attention to the completion of pendulations in equine nervous systems are helpful principles to follow when working within a gradual exposure framework as opposed to strictly doing "desensitization". That is, using subtle nervous system cues indicating the horse is deactivating and settled before moving to a higher threshold builds trust and confidence, as opposed to continuing to escalate into flooding, helplessness and shut down without resolution. Although Somatic Experiencing® has not been formally studied in use with horses (beyond informal anecdotal use) and while the author is not a professional horse trainer[4], an understanding of mammalian nervous systems and the idea of tracking the activation cycle is worth exploring further by those who are in the industry who may be curious about a neuroscience view and alternatives or ways of adapting existing approaches.

---

4    The principles proposed by the author are also largely shared by the Natural Lifemanship approach to building relationships with humans and horses, both in terms of equine-facilitated interventions but also horsemanship "training" methods promoted by Tim Jobe, a seasoned and well-respected horse professional (Jobe & Shultz-Jobe, 2016).

## 3.   Attachment as a Somatic Experience

The ability to attune accurately to what is happening supports safety in relationship because of "getting gotten" and "feeling felt" by the other. In human infants and young children, as with animals, language is not available as a way to read what is happening for the other. Instead, attunement in relationship occurs by attending and responding to somatic cues that occur in response to interactions and dynamics – whether with horses or with humans. Even when words are available, listening to the somatic current beneath the words (listening to the body story) often provides more accurate information than what has been filtered before being spoken. Attachment ruptures involve the varying degrees of misattunement that occur when relating to others (human or animal) as a result of misreading or avoiding these sociosensual and psychophysiological cues. The repair of these ruptures is an important part of renegotiating trust and security in connection. When misattunements occur without repair, this reinforces the neuroception in horses and in humans that relationships are not safe, along with the subsequent experiences of ambivalence, anxiety, avoidance, or confusion about how to respond in relationship.

Bowlby (1958) describes the nature of the attachment of young mammals (including humans and other animals) as comprised of various components, including the importance of a caregiver being a safe haven (showing responsive attunement to the child's needs); a secure base (knowing that the caregiver will be there to come back to when out exploring the world); as well as proximity seeking for safety, soothing and nourishment; and separation distress from the caregiver as source of survival. One particularly potent way of working with these components involves tracking the activation associated with how we arrive and depart in relationships. When there is insecure attachment, either closeness or separation can be activating depending on the organism's attachment experiences. Some humans or horses show evidence of discomfort with closeness and touch (such as bracing, rigidity, aversion movements, resisting/avoiding, disconnecting, fidgeting, or tense expressions and gestures, and so on), while others show evidence of discomfort when there is physical distance (appeasement, clinging, protesting, resisting, anxiety, acting out, shutting down, or stonewalling/avoidance/ disconnecting, etc.). This activation can even arise in relation to the thought of or anticipation of closeness or distance. Being able to help build a human's and horse's window of tolerance with regards to attachment and detachment helps build the capacity for relationship as well as grows the ability to feel connected to another even when not physically close. When we attune to the subtle somatic responses that occur in relationship that indicate where a human or animal is at in the activation cycle, and respond appropriately and consistently, a different experience of relationship is felt. This sets the foundation of relational repair, which can in turn result in deactivation as neuroception begins to detect evidence of safety, the nervous system becomes more regulated, and the conditions for secure attachment begin to fall into place.

Security in relationship is further enhanced by our ability to recognize where we ourselves are on the activation cycle map when interacting with others. As facilitators in equine-assisted interventions, or when working with our animals within horsemanship activities, being able to attend to our own sensations, impulses, emotions, neuroception, and activation patterns is crucial in order to provide a source of co-regulation for the humans and equines we are engaging with. Although one of the advantages of equine-assisted interventions is that human participants may find it easier to relate and attach to the animals, there is nonetheless a goal of restoring security in human relationships as well in order to increase safety and functionality in society. This requires the ability to hold space through our therapeutic presence, a foundation of secure attachment. The caregiver's ability to monitor and modulate their own arousal helps them to not cross boundaries by projecting inappropriately onto others and creating re-enactments that are reminiscent of a participant's early attachment dilemmas (having to regulate a parent, having to sublimate their own needs and emotions to prevent rejection, and so on). Recognizing when we are personally triggered by something that is happening with a human participant, a horse, their interaction, our interaction with them, or our interaction with any co-facilitators allows us to address any potential counter-transference before it externalizes and impacts the emotional safety of those around us (a skill that also relates to horsemanship approaches and being with horses in general). Tracking our own activation is related to neuroception, Porges' term for an organism's ability to detect safety, danger, or life threat and to respond accordingly. Neuroception in mammals is honed in relationship, where we look to our tribe or herd for evidence about environmental conditions and how to react. As described by Kain and Terrell (2016), the basic underlying question can be simplified to whether something is a snake or a stick – determining the difference requires having other trustworthy nervous systems around us at early stages in development whose perception is accurate. This helps us to know at an implicit level if it is safe or necessary to approach or if it is best to retreat. However, when this is not possible, or when others or our life experiences have taught us that the outside world is unsafe or not to trust our perception of things, neuroception can go awry. Neuroception can either become hyper-aroused, stuck on "on", always responding as though there was danger or life threat, even when there is no evidence to support this (false positives, "everything is a snake"), or hypo-aroused, stuck on "off", and never perceiving danger or threat in spite of evidence to support it (false negatives, "there are no snakes"). How we interact with one another, including the subtlety of our expressions, posture, movement and gestures, can further reinforce a sense of threat (and activation) or support a sense of safety (and settling) in relationship, which is true across species. In fact, horses are known to be able to recognize facial expressions not only in other horses, but also in humans, an ability previously only documented in dogs. In a recent study by Smith, Proops, Grounds, Wathan and McComb (2016), horses were found to be able to differentiate between positive and negative human emotions, showing greater sympathetic activation in response to photographs showing humans with angry expressions. Similar to people, this response pattern may even be stronger in horses with past negative experiences involving humans, as a result of a process known as kindling in the human trauma literature[5]. This lends even more credence to the importance of tracking activation and neuroception states in horse-human interactions to foster emotional and physical safety for members of both species. This also speaks to another important relational principle, that we cannot control another being but we can only be responsible for

---

5   Kindling refers to the sensitization of the nervous system to subtle cues that trigger a threat response as a result of prior stressful or traumatic experiences. These cues lead the nervous system to quickly spark to a flame in service of self-protection (Post, Weiss, Smith, Li & McCann, 1997).

ourselves. Helping humans shift out of trying to control others and instead become responsible for their own behavior and responses (moving from an external to an internal locus of control) is a common goal of therapy. Tim Jobe describes this as one of his goals when building relationships with horses as well – that the human can only be responsible for his or her own responses, which include trusting the horse to also be responsible for him or herself (personal communication, October 19, 2017). This is similar to one of the foundational principles in Somatic Experiencing®: that the human therapist must hold and convey the belief that the client's body knows how to heal, which helps start to set the conditions required for the client to respond differently. Furthermore, similar to how Somatic Experiencing® unfolds with people: if the human is regulated and attuning accurately to the horse's non-verbal cues, which supports the animal to perceive safety in the relationship, the animal's nervous system is more likely to deactivate and settle, and come back down into social engagement, connection and willingness to respond to the human's requests. This differs significantly from the more common practice of avoiding noticing one's internal states and activation and instead focusing externally and trying to control the animal, triggering neuroception of danger or threat and associated survival energy like fight, flight, freeze, shutdown and compliance as a way to get the job done. Just as good therapy is about setting the conditions of safety and security to support healing in the client and their capacity for relationship (as opposed to fixing the client), so too is good horsemanship about setting the conditions to support "healing" (regulation and connection) in the horse, trusting that the horse too will respond differently when the conditions are different.

Re-patterning neuroception also requires the caregiver, trainer or facilitator's ability to activate and deactivate appropriately in response to internal and external stimuli (such as responding without fear, judgment, or shame towards one's own feelings, sensations, needs, impulses, reactions and those of others), in order to help remap what is safe, dangerous or life threatening and respond more effectively in the moment. The more we are able to weather our own internal storms with equanimity, the more we are able to be with the activation of others, which in turn supports regulation, settling, curiosity and connection – that is, helping shift from activation to deactivation back down to social engagement in the activation cycle. As stated by Levine and Kline (2007), and adapted for the context of equine-assisted interventions (and equally relevant to horse training),

*The way to develop a calm adult presence is through experiential exercises that increase your ability to restore equilibrium, quickly and naturally, so that you are more likely to experience grace under pressure. Once your body learns "what goes up" [activation] must come down [deactivation], you are on the way to a more resilient nervous system that can weather the ups and downs of life [...] Through the mechanism of body language, facial expression and tone of voice, your own nervous system communicates directly with the [participants' and animals'] nervous systems. But before we attune to [their] sensations, rhythms and emotions, we must learn to attune to our own (p. 85).*

Tracking the somatic experience of the activation cycle and attachment relationship is not only useful in equine-assisted interventions, but may help inform negative reinforcement strategies as used in various natural horsemanship approaches. Natural horsemanship has suffered from a negative reputation in recent years by those who have seen its methods applied in ways that result in increased fear activation, learned helplessness, submissive compliance, dissociation and shutdown, resulting in many individuals turning towards positive reinforcement as an alternative and avoiding pressure-release methods altogether. Yet many also find negative reinforcement to have been very successful with their own horses, where the horses are more responsive, connected in relationship and have wider windows of tolerance. One possible explanation for the wide range of outcomes with negative reinforcement is the subtlety around the timing and intensity of pressure-release. If negative reinforcement methods:

- are used with an understanding of the components of secure attachment (safe haven, secure base, and the nuances of working with activation associated with approaching and distancing)

- incorporate tracking behavioral evidence of where a horse is in the activation cycle[6]

---

6 That is, are they socially engaged, experiencing tolerable stress arousal and still connected, engaging in active defensive responses or management strategies to cope, in freeze, or in deactivation and settling?

- work in a titrated way with incrementally larger thresholds of activation and deactivation (that is, starting small and increasing requests from there)
- wait for pendulations of activation-deactivation to complete before proceeding (that is, timing pressure-release with where the horse is at in the activation cycle)

– this might result in more positive outcomes.

In other words, instead of a common re-enactment of learned helplessness, shut down and compliance to be in relationship with the owner/trainer, the experience might instead constitute a renegotiation of working through optimal levels of stress response while retaining a sense of connection (remaining socially engaged), resulting in a wider window of tolerance, trust and confidence. This does not mean that attending to this type of information will be easy, as reading horse body language is subject to interpretation and misattunements will certainly occur, as they do in human relationships. However, coming back to these principles and maps may provide new opportunities for repair in the horse-human relationship and starting places to begin again. If these are principles used in building healthy relationships with humans and in trauma therapy with humans, which are founded on an understanding of how mammalian nervous systems function and how mammals are relational creatures, then these principles are also applicable to equines as well. This is especially true when bringing horsemanship groundwork methods into equine-assisted interventions, in particular with trauma survivors, who are sensitive to coercion and power and control dynamics in relationship. How healing is it for a client to have to dominate a horse through methods that induce psychological control in order to achieve an outcome? Again, the aim is for renegotiation as opposed to a potentially traumatic re-enactment.

Tracking the subtleties of the activation cycle in horses may be facilitated by the recent work of Wathan, Burrows, Waller and McComb (2015), who created the Equine Facial Action Coding System. This categorization of body language in horses describes all possible facial expressions and movements related to emotional expression (for a total of 17 compared to 27 in humans, with a number of them corresponding to one another) and was found to be easily learned and applied with a high degree of accuracy even by individuals without horse experience. This study provides evidence that reading equine body language is not a talent reserved for a few but a skill that can be honed as a tool to improve horse-human relationships.

Attending to the somatic and attachment features of what is transpiring in the context of equine-human interactions in general, and in particular of equine-assisted interventions and horsemanship methods, helps build new neural templates for safety and security, regulation, and relationship. Regardless of the kind of equine-assisted model or training approach being used, these principles can be integrated as an additional lens through which to view what is happening. Whether one is engaged in activities that are more directive and focus on doing things with horses, or more non-directive and focus on being with horses, or anywhere in between, this perspective can yield rich new opportunities and avenues of exploration. Further research on the integration of these principles and frameworks into equine-assisted interventions and horsemanship is highly encouraged.

## About the Author

Sarah Schlote, MA, RP, CCC, SEP is a registered psychotherapist, Somatic Experiencing Practitioner, and founder and director of The Refuge: Centre for Healing and Recovery and the EquuSpirit: Healing with Horses program. She is the creator of Equine-Facilitated Trauma Therapy, an integrative approach combining attachment theory, touch work, polyvagal theory, ego state work and trauma-informed care principles into equine-assisted interventions along with Somatic Experiencing® (referred to as EQUUSOMA). She completed a trauma-focused master's in Counseling Psychology, conducted her thesis research on animal- and equine-facilitated interventions, and was involved in the development of ethics and standards for AAT in Canada. She has pursued training in trauma neuroscience, mammalian stress psychophysiology, touch work, and table work, including Somatic Experiencing®, EMDR, Body Memory Recall, attachment-focused therapy, parts work for structural dissociation, trauma-focused Integrative Equine-Facilitated Wellness, nature-assisted therapy and is currently learning the foundations of Natural Lifemanship. Her work is experiential, relational, depth oriented, somatic and embodiment focused, and promotes safety, consent, choice, voice, and empowerment for all sentient beings involved. A seasoned and sought after speaker on trauma-informed care and trauma-specific therapy, Sarah is also a longstanding mindfulness practitioner, SE training assistant, and perpetual student of horsemanship.

## References


Blanc, J.J., Alboni, P., & Benditt, D.G. (2015, March 1). Vasovagal syncope in humans and protective reactions in animals. *EP Europace*, 17(3), 345-349.

Bowlby, J. (1958). The nature of the child's tie to his mother. *International Journal of Psycho-Analysis*, 39, 350-373.

Foundation for Human Enrichment (2007). *Somatic Experiencing Healing Trauma (training manual)*. Boulder, CO.

Hunter, C. (2017, October 2). When dissociation looks like cooperation. Natural Lifemanship Trainers' Blog. Published online at https://naturallifemanship.com/dissociation-looks-like-cooperation/

Jobe, T.D. & Shultz-Jobe, B.N. (2016). *Fundamentals of Natural Lifemanship: Trauma Focused Equine Assisted Psychotherapy*. Liberty Hill, TX: Natural Lifemanship.

Kain, K.L. & Terrell, S.J. (2016). Somatic Resilience and Regulation: Early Trauma [training]. Victoria, BC.

Kozlowska, K., Walker, P., McLean, L. & Carrive, P. (2015). Fear and the defense cascade: Clinical implications and management. *Harvard Review of Psychiatry*, 23(4), 263-287.

Levine, P.A. (1997). *Waking the Tiger: Healing Trauma*. Berkeley, CA: North Atlantic Books.

Levine, P.A. (2015). *Trauma and Memory*. Berkeley, CA: North Atlantic Books.

Levine, P.A. & Kline, M. (2007). *Trauma Through a Child's Eyes*. North Atlantic Books.

Payne, P. & Crane-Godreau, M.A. (2015, April 1). The preparatory set: A novel approach to understanding stress, trauma, and the bodymind therapies. *Frontiers in Human Neuroscience*, published online at: http://journal.frontiersin.org/article/10.3389/fnhum.2015.00178/full

Payne, P., Levine, P.A. & Crane-Godreau, M.A. (2015, February 4). Somatic experiencing: Using interoception and proprioception as core elements of trauma therapy. *Frontiers in Human Neuroscience*, published online at https://www.frontiersin.org/articles/10.3389/fpsyg.2015.00093/full

Post, R.M., Weiss, S.R.B., Smith, M., Li, H. & McCann, U. (1997). Kindling versus quenching: Implications for the evolution and treatment of posttraumatic stress disorder. *Annals of the New York Academy of Sciences*, 821, 285-295.

Resnick, C. (2005). *Naked Liberty*. Amigo Publications Inc.

Schlote, S. (2017). Applying a trauma lens to equine welfare. In I. Parent (Ed.), *A Horse is a Horse, of Course: Compendium From the First International Symposium of Equine Welfare and Wellness*. Createspace Independent Publishing Platform.

Schlote, S. (2018, in press). Integrating Somatic Experiencing and Attachment Theory into Equine-Facilitated Trauma Therapy. In K. Trotter and J. Baggerly (Eds.), *Equine Assisted Therapy Activities for Counselors: Harnessing Solutions to Common Problems*. Taylor & Francis.

Schlote, S. & Parent, I. (2018, in press). Treating complex dissociation through equine-assisted trauma therapy: An ego state approach. In K. Trotter and J. Baggerly (Eds.), *Equine Assisted Therapy Activities for Counselors: Harnessing Solutions to Common Problems*. Taylor & Francis.

Siegel, D.J. (1999). *The Developing Mind: How Relationships and the Brain Interact to Shape Who We Are*. New York, NY: The Guilford Press.

Smith, A.V., Proops, L., Grounds, K., Wathan, J., & McComb, K. (2016, October 4). Functionally relevant responses to human facial expressions of emotion in the domestic horse (Equus caballus). *Biology Letters*, 12, published online at: http://rsbl.royalsocietypublishing.org/content/12/2/20150907

Taylor, S.E., Klein, L.C., Lewis, B.P., Gruenewald, T.L., Gurung, R.A.R, & Updegraff, J.A. (2000). Biobehavioral responses to stress in females: Tend-and-befriend, not fight-or-flight. *Psychological Review*, 107, 441-429.

Wathan, J., Burrows, A.M., Waller, B.M., & McComb, K. (2015, August 5). EquiFACS: The equine facial coding system. *PLOSOne*, published online at: http://journals.plos.org/plosone/article?id=10.1371/journal.pone.0131738

Wright, M. (2017). *The 7 Mindful Movements: Understanding the Subtleties of Liberty Horsemanship*. Ravenna, ON: The Wright Approach.

CHAPTER 24

# Joy of Creative Writing with Horses

## Cases of Therapeutic Encounters

Pirjo Suvilehto

*Creative writing and other art-activities are experienced with the presence of equines in Northern Finland. How does an animal presence affect the poetry therapy triad of literature, facilitator, and participant? Human-animal studies focus on encounters with horses. Creative writing (CW) has been largely studied and considered as a vehicle for self-knowledge, and is used for the benefit of education and wellbeing among different age groups. There are story-crafting (Riihelä, 2001), biography research among elderly people (Brown-Wilson, Tetley, Healey & Wolton, 2011), CW in academic studies (Peary, 2015) etc. CW-process may also be assessed among horses, at the stables, where a person may study one's feelings and concepts. Horses are often seen as therapeutic animals in psychotherapy, riding therapy, and in a context of social pedagogy. In the context of CW traditional thoughts and roles may have been challenged.*

This article includes examples of cases, how CW and horses may benefit self-expression and growth, and aid in the context of poetry therapy. Theory is based on literature and theories of CW (expressive writing by Pennebaker 2004), and post humanist theories like human-animal studies, and McCarthy-Hynes and Hynes-Perry (1986/1994) as with biblio/poetry therapy. Method is literature-based. Results suggest that CW and equine as a combination is a rewarding tool for increasing self-expression and thus sensitive toward self-knowledge and self-esteem. Art-activities alongside horse-contacts create a new and fascinating combination, in which both human and animals may share the same space and also the experience of wellbeing. New skills are activated, emotions and self-expression are expressed, and insights are gained.

## 1.  Introduction

Two ponies are approaching a group of early childhood education students. The ponies are eagerly bending their heads towards the students as if wishing them welcome. The Polish pony Etola goes to each of these eight students, saying "hello", and then the ponies go to the field to eat hay. We have come to a private stable of two ponies, where different cases and groups of art-based horse-activities (AHA) have been assessed for two years.

Students have arrived at the stable to begin a new university course of 25 ECT, and to get to know each other. Students are a bit unsure as to the purpose for coming to the countryside and driving 35 kilometers from the university campus, just to see the ponies. After a two-hour-meeting they are reassured that this was a great idea. And they are impressed by how social and sensitive these ponies can be to strangers like them. That is surely a great example to take into account and to be remembered when students are later about to meet new children and their parents in an immigration reception center. Students will later be running a children's club for asylum seekers in a Finnish immigration reception center in Northern Finland; and this is just a beginning of the process. First, they need to be friends with each other and with the horses. Horses are here to be a reminder of something authentic, something natural, something happening right now and right here, like the concept of mindfulness. This meeting with ponies is also a reminder of something new, maybe even a bit scary for those who have not been with a big animal like a horse. This is about to provide new ideas, joy, togetherness, the experience of nature. Some of them even wished to make closer contact with these ponies.

There are many cases to consider. One case involves children in a pony club, another case involves a five-month-period of bibliotherapy at the stable, and another involves an infant with her mother. The primary attendees in this kind of work with ponies and art-activities vary from a 4,5-month-infant to adults and the horse-activities are considered as metaphoric working.

The theoretical approach in this research and horse-art-activities comes from the field of creative therapies, especially bibliotherapy, from which I wrote my doctoral thesis (2008) and later research. The role of the equine may be seen as a silent co-fellow, like a metaphor to many situations and feelings. Their function is also as the representation of nature, as they are big animals with their own instincts and moments of fear and joy. A horse always needs a companion, and this is, at the same time, both a special and an important and obvious consideration for sessions with the clients. The theoretical approach used, when working together with horses and human, lies mostly in natural horsemanship accompanied by the perspectives of psychoanalysis.

## 2. Theory of Human-Animal Studies

Human-animal studies focus on encounters with horses. Scientific research on horses is plentiful and is a fascinating research field which ranges from riding sports to the field of dealing with emotional challenges, such as in equine assisted psychotherapy (EFP). Studies (Lentini & Knox, 2015; Gibbons, Cunningham, Katelyn, Poelker & Chajón, 2016) have demonstrated the extraordinary sensitivity of horses to human feelings and emotions. A horse can serve to mirror feelings of the people surrounding them. Secondly, by nature, horses are both herd and prey animals, and these qualities predispose them not only to being sensitive to nonverbal behavior, but to looking for and expecting leadership from others. Thirdly, the size of a horse means that it cannot readily be forced to act; humans must use other means to elicit his cooperation and desired behavior. Learning to direct the behavior of such a large animal can potentially decrease fearfulness and increase self-confidence. (Gibbons, Cunningham, Paiz, Poelker & Chajón, 2016.) In horse-assisted psychotherapy, horses are equal members of the team: there are two- and four-legged team members instead of humans and horses. In this kind of therapy horses have the same choices, rights, needs, and wishes as people have. That is, there is an understanding of "not instrumentalizing" the horses. (Parent, 2016.)

Human-animal studies research emphasizes the multiplicity and variety of human contact with animals. Animals are supportive and are a means of therapy in Animal-Assisted Therapy (AAT), especially in Equine Assisted Therapy. Gehrke's (2009) study emphasizes how therapeutic interventions with horses may improve the mental state and the somatic system of humans during various states of interaction.

Some university programs have developed Equine Assisted Learning (EAL), where horses do the work of teaching and healing through a variety of equine assisted applications (Salem, 2001). Each of these professional groups has a different type of certification and theoretical background. Equine-facilitated experiential learning (EFEL) approaches the field from a learning perspective and emphasizes the equine as a partner (Lentini & Knox, 2015). Among horses there are different emphases in Equine-assisted activities and -therapies. Yet research, particularly on the discipline of equine facilitated mental health (documenting the beneficial effect horses have on human), is lacking.

Recently, the combination of humanities and animals has been of interest to Finnish researchers (see Leinonen, 2016; Aaltola, 2004, 2013). A good pedagogical activity involving horses would be to make art-activities WITH horses instead of USING horses as tools, as is often the case in the professional field among those people who work with horses. In post-qualitative research (Lather & Perre, 2013) "big data" or convincing tables are not needed to ensure that an item is accurate; On the contrary, there are many minor points that are both interesting and worth exploring. Empirical generalizations are not necessarily needed. Instead, a careful and detailed case study can promote theoretical generalization.

## 3.   Theory of Bibliotherapy

In biblio/poetry therapy, literature is used as a vehicle for therapeutic interaction between a participant and a facilitator, having the main goal of promoting mental health (Mc Carthy Hynes & Hynes-Berry 1994/1986, 910). Poetry therapy is effective in different age-groups, with a different emphasis in many areas (Lutovac & Kaasila, 2011; Pardeck, 2013/1998; Pennebaker, 2004; Suvilehto, 2016; 2008). Analyzing art, writing, dreams, and other expressive items in the field of psychotherapy has become well recognized as a part of the available research methods (Sharf, 2012/2004, 622630). Writings imply inner states of minds and may increase the willingness and ability to express oneself in an appropriate way (Suvilehto, 2008). This is especially assumed to be the goal in poetry/biblio/writing therapy (Mazza, 2003). The process of biblio/poetry therapy has been studied and a number of different steps have been identified. McCarthy Hynes's and Hynes-Berry's (1994/1986, 4259) process of bibliotherapy is a four-step-model. The steps are:

- recognition,
- examination,
- juxtaposition, and
- application to the self.

The process involves raising a person's feeling-responses and thus leading to the release of feelings or insights related to self-understanding (McCarthy Hynes & Hynes-Berry, 1994/1986, 43).

*Recognition (step 1)* means that the participant finds something interesting in the material that captures her/his attention. That "something" might, for example, be a person or a description of an experience just read (McCarthy Hynes & Hynes-Berry, 1994/1986, 4445). In this first stage the person might recognize patterns of responses related to a text, or discussions, or emotions etc. If a catharsis occurs in a person's response, she/he will be able to release thoughts or feelings that have been suppressed. This emotional release may come from a strong identification with something in the work, and may also be about how this "something" touches a buried memory or emotion. So the term catharsis, in this context, means a profound experience of recognition, which may take an issue and discussions of the issue to a whole different and personal level (McCarthy Hynes & Hynes-Berry, 1994/1986, 4647). Catharsis and other kinds of recognition may occur in the first step of the process. At times, the recognition will come through a spontaneous emotional response depicted in literature. Recognition in bibliotherapy may occur if the literature offered is universal enough, beautiful enough, or profound but true enough to touch the reader; and may, in a group of individuals, raise a discussion (McCarthy Hynes & Hynes-Berry, 1994/1986, 48).

*Examination (step 2)* means exploring the feeling-responses that have been aroused and recognized by the literature and by the discussions. Examination raises the questions who, what, when, why, how, how much, and wherefore. The facilitator tries to get the members of the group to examine their reactions for themselves by posing further questions that deepen and make the issue that has just been recognized even more personal (McCarthy Hynes & Hynes-Berry, 1994/1986, 4950).

*Juxtaposition (step 3)* means going back to step one and the original reaction to the material, but this time in the light of input. This step forces a deeper examination of the issues involved. This means, for example, that the person may look at a thing differently than before. The juxtaposition may trigger a recognition that the first idea or sensation was not valid at all. In this stage a person can examine certain issues and realizes, that:

- the literature may correct discrepancies,
- the literature may offer role-model possibilities, and
- the literature may depict alternatives

(McCarthy Hynes & Hynes-Berry, 1994/1986, 5052).

*Application to Self (step 4)* means ending the process through evaluation and integration. By now the feelings and concepts have been recognized, examined, and juxtaposed and now it is time for them to become genuinely experienced. Evaluation means that the participant makes a personal commitment by using the new attitudes. In other words, the insights are integrated. The person's self-awareness has been developing throughout the previous three steps and the last step may raise the question "Am I willing to change?". Both the evaluation and a commitment to change, to take steps toward growth will take time, even years (McCarthy Hynes & Hynes-Berry, 1994/1986, 5253). In bibliotherapy it is the participant who must recognize, examine, juxtapose, and integrate feeling-responses and the understandings, although the facilitator may help to find these. To be able to gain these steps, the participant should be able to analyze issues, to take an honest look at the inner self, to have enough objectivity to view a feeling or behavior pattern from another perspective, and to have adequate hope and self-confidence to make the changes that are needed (McCarthy Hynes & Hynes-Berry, 1994/1986, 58).

## 4. Equine-Human Well-Being and Togetherness

The basis of the horse-activities, held at the stables in these cases, lies in the idea of cozy art-activities with two ponies, Pritney, a charming young Shetland pony, and Etola, a more mature Polish pony. Etola has served earlier, in her previous riding school, as a confident pony for disabled customers. Pritney as a typical Shetland pony is sensitive, eloquent, and accustomed to children. She also seems to like different play-activities with children. In these social meetings and art-activities these ponies are allowed to be themselves, as their own equine-persons. When an attendant comes to a field to take photos of them, the ponies may decide whether they stay there or go away. Both humans and animals are supposed to be enjoying their moments as participants. Ponies can be at liberty with us, while we are having sessions with art-activities like writing in the field, or painting, or having discussions near the ponies.

There are different, short, art-based happenings in the milieu of these ponies: acoustic concerts at the front yard; a course for facilitators and social workers on how to use creative writing to enhance wellbeing; having visitors from the disabled unit; having teamwork sessions with the university students of early childhood education; or having child club meetings.

Both ponies' welfare and well-being before, during and after the human-horse interaction are solid, since there are no requirements towards them except for being there to be seen, to be hugged, to be caressed, and to have delicate contacts with people. The ponies are free to attend or not to attend the art-actions. The ponies were there to be touched, brushed and looked at, and they were allowed to be free to approach us, to follow us, to look at us, even to touch us. The ponies appeared to be tranquil and slow in their silent and peaceful appearance.

## 5.   Equine Moments

In a case of a five-month-period with one attendant, a young lady, writing sessions are happening at the stables once a month. The idea about the equine and the significance of horses lies in a creation process and how it manifests itself there. A person may write about horses, or may not include them in stories, pictures, or poems. It is not necessary to mention a horse in a piece of writing or even in a discussion. The value of the horse may be silent and without words. The interpretation is thus to identify and to describe how things happen and what progress there is. To see and feel the presence of these two ponies is to gain a deeper understanding of one's own feelings and thoughts. One need not talk of one's traumas or therapeutic needs.

A creative writing task can be as simple as to write something titled "If I was a horse" and then feel the joy of experiencing it through words. At the same time, the images may move to real ponies that the writer sees at the moment. W1 wrote about her impressions as a horse. This poem is energetic, joyful, and playful, especially when the protagonist of the poem says, "I would be Faster than the breeze." One single poem may take the reader into the deep and up into the sky in one short moment. This may also be the power of this method.

*"If I was a horse?*
*I would be warm-blooded Arabian.*
*I would be gamboling in the grass, and be enjoying the horse's life. I would munch on carrots.*

*I would be like a wind, which blows.*
*Like a shooting star.*
*I would be Faster than the breeze."*

In a writer's stick figure -drawing of a relationship with a horse there are two figures in contact together. The stick pony is standing facing the stick figure, and an interaction is now possible. The stick figure has no face, so everything is "clean" and empty in the beginning. After this drawing the writer asks, "what is the purpose of this drawing task? What analysis can be drawn from this picture?" After this there are discussions of whether everything needs to be interpreted, or whose interpretation is the right one etc. There could be a thought that the contact with these two figures in the drawing is promising and interactive. The stick pony wants to approach the stick figure, because the figure's arms are open.

An equine moment may be as simple as browsing a horse magazine. Or, it may be a caressing moment with ponies and brushing their hair. When the writer met the ponies for the first time, she spontaneously commented: "Oh, how gentle they are. So communicative and social." And, "Pritney is so cute, and Etola so sensitive. Pritney is a princess and Etola is a Cinderella," (W2, 19.2.2016). The writer creates a relationship with an animal and "reads" the pony: One moment the larger pony, Etola, flinched a bit in reaction to the writer's sudden swaying, and immediately she said aloud that the horse had reacted to her. In psychotherapeutic interaction reality begins to become realized in a moment and also finds symbolic ways to be expressed. The situation needs to allow for sharing and mutual understanding (Siltala, 2007, 384). After this shared moment, the writer offers an apple to the ponies. When Etola approaches the writer, she glances at her and whispers "oh, dear," to this pony.

This study has been a short glimpse of different cases of art-based horse-activities at the private stable of two ponies in Northern Finland in 2015-2017. Encounters with humans and animals are always private, interactive, and with ethical considerations. A therapeutic moment may be as simple as a pony willing to stay together, in a circle, with a group of university students discussing how they have felt during the visit to the stables. And Etola-pony willing to be part of the ending discussion – by its own, free will, in an intention to feel and, I think, like silently saying, without words: we are the same group.

## About the Author

Pirjo Suvilehto, Docent of Literature, PhD, is an accomplished literature and childhood scholar at the University of Oulu, Finland. She is also an author, and has published over 25 books. Her latest interest is in the field of arts-based horse activities (AHA), a method which she has created and used in the context of bibliotherapy and animals. With her own dear "my little ponies" Pritney and Etola, she has combined developmental bibliotherapy and animal-assisted arts practices to enhance joy and wellbeing. Since the publication of her PhD thesis, which was the first academic doctoral thesis in the field of children's and adolescents' bibliotherapy in Finland, Suvilehto continued an intensive research career to the extent that she was awarded the title of Docent. In their statements, the external evaluators highlighted the originality and scientific innovativeness of her research. She has also been holding lectures on bibliotherapy (Armenian State Pedagogical University, Yerevan, Armenia 2016 and promoting counseling and courses in the field of literature, creative writing and bibliotherapy). She has presented her research in international and national conferences and seminars (e.g. EECERA, Arts in Society, Conference of Animal Studies), given lectures on the subject, made public appearances on radio and TV, and popularized her research by publishing a vast amount of shorter writings in newspapers and journals as a critic and expert. She has been a confident member of Finnish Literature Therapy Association, and Finnish Youth Research Society's Publishing Committee for many years. She has been awarded membership in Finnish in the Children's and Youth Author's Association. She is a member of a board of Finnish Society for Human-Animal Studies.

# References


Aaltola, E. (2004). Eläimen moraalinen arvo. Helsinki: Vastapaino.

Aaltola, E. (2013). Johdatus eläinfilosofiaan (Ed.). Helsinki: Gaudeamus.

Brown-Wilson, C. B. , Tetley, J. , Healey, J. & Wolton, R. (2011). The Best Care Is Like Sunshine: Accessing Older People's Experiences of Living in Care Homes Through Creative Writing. *Activities, Adaptation & Aging*, 35(1) pp. 120. Published online: 14 Mar 2011.

Gehrke, E. (2010). *Narha's Studies*. pp. 2023.

Gehrke, E. (2009). Developing Coherent Leadership in Partnership with Horses - A New Approach to Leadership. *Journal of Research in Innovative Teaching*, 2.

Gibbons, J. L., Cunningham, Catherine A., Paiz, L., Poelker, K. E. & Chajón, A. (2016). Now, he will be the leader of the house: An equine intervention with at-risk Guatemalan youth, *International Journal of Adolescence and Youth*, DOI: 10.1080/02673843.2016.1202844 To link to this article: http://dx.doi.org/10.1080/02673843.2016.1202844 Read 12.7.2016.

Lather, P. & ST. Pierre, E.A. (2013). Post-Qualitative Research. *International journal of qualitative studies in education*, 26(6)629633. http://dx.doi.org/10.1080/09518398.2013.788752DOI

Leinonen, R-M. (2016). From Servant to Therapist: *The Changing Meaning of Horses in Finland. The Meaning of Horses - Biosocial Encounters*. Ed. Dona Davis & Anita Maurstad. Routledge, 54-68.

Lentini, J. A. & Knox, M. S. (2015). Equine-Facilitated Psychotherapy with Children and Adolescents: *An Update and Literature Review Journal of Creativity in Mental Health* Vol. 10, Iss. 3, pages 278305 DOI: 10.1080/15401383.2015.1023916

Lutovac, S. & Kaasila, R. (2011). *Beginning a pre-service teacher's mathematical identity work through narrative rehabilitation and bibliotherapy. Teaching in Higher Education*. 16(2)225236.

Mazza, N. (2012). Poetry/creative writing for an arts and athletics community outreach program for at-risk youth. *Journal of Poetry therapy*. 225231 http://dx.doi.org/10.1080/08893675.2012.738491

Mazza, N. (2003). *Poetry therapy: theory and practice*. Brunner Routledge, 2003. ISBN 0- 415-94486-4.

McCarthy Hynes, A. & Hynes-Berry, M. (1994/1986). *Biblio/Poetry Therapy. The Interactive Process. A Handbook*. North Star Press of St Cloud. East Peoria Illinois: Versa Press.

Pardeck, J. A. (2013/1998). *Using Books in Clinical Social Work Practice: A Guide to Bibliotherapy*. New York: Routledge.

Parent. I. (2016). Instrumentalizing horses. 30.5.2016. Ilka Parent4s Linkedin. Read 2.11.2016.

Peary, A. (2016). The Terrain of Prewriting. *The Journal of Creative Writing Studies*. Vol 2(1) http://scholarworks.rit.edu/jcws/vol2/iss1/1 17.9.2016

Peary, A. (2015). The Pedagogy of Creative Writing across the curriculum. In: *Creative Writing pedagogies for the Twenty-First Century*. Ed. A. Peary & T. C. Hunley. Southern Illinois University. Carbondale. p. 194220. SIU Press. Read 29.9.2016.

Pennebaker, J. W. 2010. Expressive writing in a clinical setting. Independent practitioner p. 2325. http://citeseerx.ist.psu.edu/viewdoc/download;jsessionid=8CF3DF65812C0226C858E CBFF4D3DDA2?doi=10.1.1.307.8403&rep=rep1&type=pdf Read 16.10.2016

Pennebaker, J.W. (2004). *Writing to heal: A guided journal for recovering from trauma and emotional upheaval.* Oakland, CA: New Harbinger Press.

Riihelä, M. (2001). The story crafting method & the story crafting video. http://www.edu.helsinki.fi/ lapsetkertovat/english/Riihela_Storycrafting_method_and_videoMR. PDF loaded 15.10.2016

Salem, P. (2001). What is Equine Assisted Learning. Retrieved from http://horsesteachingandhealing. com/different-ea-models/

Sharf, R. S. 2012/2004. *Theories of Psychotherapy and Counseling: Concepts and Cases*, 5th Edition. Belmont: Brooks/Cole, Cengage Learning

Siltala, P. (2007). Kolmen seinävaatteen arvoitus – skitsofrenian nimetön. Teoksessa: Askelista jotka otamme. *Psykoanalyyttisia esseitä* s. 295214. Helsinki: Therapeia.

Suvilehto, P. (2016). Horror and aggression in childrens creative writing: implications for bibliotherapy and child development, *Journal of Poetry Therapy.* http://dx.doi.org/10.1080/08893675.2016.1176159

Suvilehto, P. (2008). Lasten luova kirjoittaminen psyykkisen tulpan avaajana. Tapaustutkimus Pohjoissuomalaisen sairaalakoulun ja Päätalo-instituutin 8–13-vuotiaiden lasten kirjoituksista. Kirjallisuuden väitöstutkielma. Humanistinen tiedekunta. Acta Universitatis Ouluensis. B Humaniora 83. Suvilehto, Pirjo, Creative writing as an opener of children's emotional blocks. A case study of the writings of children aged 8–13 attending a Northern Finnish hospital school and Päätalo Institute

CHAPTER 25

# A Horse is a Horse, of Course – Heart Connection

Eva Balzer

*Open the door to your heart – I'd like to invite you to a little journey:*

*Imagine you are a horse – a living being that is meant to live in a herd, to move around many miles per day. Being able to live from hardly anything, a bit of grass and herbs – whatever nature offers at that moment. Being able to find your own water resources, raise your children, form and live in a team, build relationships, being extremely sensitive and being able to communicate on a high level even without the spoken word. Sense the difference between a lion who is hungry and wants to eat you and a lion who just wants to have a sip of water. Imagine you are a horse, a living being that does not get depressed or burned out because you know your own space, your level of energy and your caches and you know and accept your place in your horse society. How wise is that? And now imagine you are a horse and you meet human beings. They want to tell you who you are, what you want, how you feel; they want to save you and help you. They put you in boxes, wrap you in blankets and give you tons to eat. And they do all that with the best intention but without asking for your opinion. How does that feel? Do you understand the message behind the scene? Do you understand what these human beings really want? And you are still patient, loving and always a good friend! Thank you!*

*Description of the "horse" e.g. sentient, reactive, flight animal, herd animal, social abilities, cognitive abilities, learning abilities, biological abilities, etc.*

I am looking at the horse as a living being, bearing in mind that it is categorized as a prey animal that lives in a strong social structure with male and female horses. It is the natural instinctive behavior as a flight animal that, in order to survive, it chooses to run away rather than to attack somebody as defense. This is what happens at a distance when the horse has the choice of space. Once the predator is too close to the horse and the horse cannot choose the flight mode anymore, it chooses to move toward the predator in order to have a slight chance for survival.

Horses are sentient beings, open and curious animals that are fast learners. They have the ability to read others within seconds. Many times I have seen people who thought they have trained their horses but from a different perspective I could see that, in reality, the horse had trained its person in a very subtle way.

My focus right now is the social herd structure, the horses' ability to adjust to situations easily and balance themselves, or more precisely, their individual needs and energy with the needs and energy of the herd at the same time. It appears that their energy level is highly efficient if they are not interrupted by humans.

Why am I writing that? Because I honestly think that if we could get over ourselves and trust these beautiful intelligent creatures more, our partnerships would grow and thrive in a way that we cannot imagine.

As I said, I am working with my horses and their herd structure in a way that reflects the strong togetherness of the horse society, as well as the strengths and abilities that each individual gives to the herd.

I am looking at the herd model with regard to the horses within the herd and the ability of the herd to balance itself and adjust to new situations.

*Description of the theoretical approach in this article; description of the horses' role/function and responsibility in equine assisted/facilitated therapy/approach/intervention.*

My Heart Connection work is based on the Epona approach of Linda Kohanov, the HEAL model taught by Leigh Shambo and Kathleen Barry Ingram, and adding my own leadership experience as a manager in a global company, my knowledge of 14 years alternative healing methods and my family constellation work. And last, but not least, my experience being a sentient person myself.

I regard my job as being the facilitator of the get-together of horses and humans in a safe environment and being the guide through a process step by step. I am also responsible for the transfer process that occurs during the horse time and how to use it in the "outside" world. I am the translator from horse into human language as a coach versus an interpreter.

What do I need for this relation?

First of all a few rational completely unromantic questions:

There is no right or wrong – just a decision and negotiation in the moment.

I need to know who I am – what do I want? What are my shadow sides? Who am I when I am authentic? What are my boundaries?

Who is my partner – in this case the horse? What is its character/type? What is the breed, what is its story, what are his needs?

Some horses are playful; others are not. Some horses need more clarity than others. Some more guidance and ground rules. A helpful reminder for me is the question: what is the behavior my horse shows instead of who is he? A behavior can change depending on the person he works with.

I am not a friend of methods as I feel that methods bring you away from your feelings. At the same time, I acknowledge that using a method is giving a bit of structure and safety. I prefer clear rules and safety instructions. Some people like to work with a halter others do not. There is no right or wrong. If the horse and the person feel comfortable in that situation that is where to go, and then you can open up the space.

As a coach, I feel responsible for being present and "outside" of the situation – I am the one in charge!

Special focus on leadership skills:

Mindful "leadership" versus who moves whom?! Does it really matter who moves whom? Does this really tell you who is the boss? I personally think that is very narrow minded.

Before I dive into "real" leadership training, I focus on one question:

Because leadership, to me, means that you are able to lead yourself in the first place. The question is: Do you know yourself?

Do you know your strengths and weaknesses? Are you aware of your talents? Are you able to decide what you really want and what you do not want in order to say yes and no? Are you ready to stop drama and live authentically?

Can you balance your energy level for the sake of all beings? Do you know your physical and psychological boundaries?

Are you ready to be your own leader before you go ahead and lead others?

Mostly in team workshops or in leadership trainings, the "real agenda" is about developing your personality and daring to live that and taking the lead.

Horses find any hidden agenda! If you really want to know what the issue is, go to the horses.

One next step – what's leadership about? Somebody once said the relationship about horses is seen as who moves who – is that true? Or is it one next step – the courage that the horse touches you inside and touches your true feelings and your heart?

Or – could we have both? Allow the horse to touch your heart and your feelings, and also be able to be centered and comfortable in knowing yourself, that you can allow the horse to move you. You can also move the horse – both come from the place of true connection, but actually neither needs to be right or wrong or judged as there is no ego at play, or agenda of making the horse do anything, or needing to prove either scenario.

*Description of the theoretical approach you use when working with horses and humans (i.e. Person Centered, Psychoanalytic, Cognitive-Behavioral for mental health, or Natural Horsemanship, Liberty Training, etc. for Equine Specialists); the primary population group you work with and the framework you use with that population group*

General thoughts on EFL work:

I have done quite a few horse leadership and team trainings.

The elements of these trainings were:

- "Walk like a leader" – you work with a rope and halter on the horse and ask it follow you around the hall, across some obstacles.

- After a while I thought this was stupid and not authentic. Any well-educated horse will follow with a certain technique. Work with the client and it will work. It did not feel right to me and now I am not using this method. Still I can see the benefit for the client. Many inexperienced people are proud to be able to move 500 kg after some time and they grow with this experience; and most horses do not mind that – maybe – because it is every day business to them. There is no right or wrong when both parties feel comfortable in that situation.

- "Herding" – you work as a team together and try to move horses from A to B without touching them and without using tools.

- "Classical round pen join up" – very YANG driven approach based on the theory of Monty Roberts. I hardly ever see people who are able to work in a YIN driven approach, meaning to catch the horse's attention without pushing, driving it away or using treats but by engaging the horse and inviting it to follow you.

The benefits for humans – it is quite impressive for many people to "lead" a horse without a rope. Self-confidence grows and there is a loss of fear of the unknown. I have seen many people who have grown a lot in these workshops, who have realized how they are seen from the outside world and who have started to understand the concept of energy and nonverbal communication.

But what is the price the horses pay?

FLIP THE COIN – Most horse watchers were men and they have their glasses on; maybe we are missing a few pieces when we only follow that thread? Most horsemen are men. They see the world with their eyes and social background. I do not know any women who have lived with horses, studied them and published what they have learned.

Dressage came originally from wartime. Horses were the soldiers' partners and had to listen without discussions. In Western riding, you need work horses as a partner who can assess situations and you need to rely on them.

So from today's point of view – where is the YIN aspect? The female approach? To nurture horses, to care for them, to wait and to see and to "pull" aspect without a rope?

I mainly work in 1:1 sessions or in small groups right now; no special group but people from all areas who feel the need to change something.

It is rather a person-centered constellation work process; a highly energetic, nonverbal approach. My favorite models are the Johari window where we make the blind spot visible, touchable and adjustable. Plus, the Karpman drama triangle where I am aiming to move from drama into the authentic circle by gaining the individual's own power, and by looking at situations from a distant but not dissociated perspective.

I work a lot around the awareness of your thoughts versus your body awareness and the consciousness about your feelings and emotions.

*Description of why you work with horses/why they are part of your team when working with people/clients, with focus on the horses' roles, functions, positions and abilities within that role/function/position*

Why do I work with horses?

Is it not time to open the door of our hearts and thus open up the opportunity to start a whole new relationship between horses and humans?

I did not grow up with horses, but I was always interested in them and drawn to them when I saw them. I started riding in my late twenties, bought one horse, read Linda Kohanov's *Riding between the Worlds*, and went to the EFL training of Leigh Shambo and Kathleen Barry Ingram HEAL. One of the HEAL keys is to measure the arousal level of my clients and to do a body scan. I do both with myself to check where I am and what I pick up from my clients. I need to know where they are before we start working with the horses, to check whether they are in their body or their head.

It is quite simple: I myself have experienced a lot. I was diagnosed with PTSD, severe trauma, burn out, depression.

I went through many different stages of therapy and coaching...

The work that helped me most was the work with the horses because, to me, it is the softest and most respectful work I have gone through. At the same time, it is grounded, honest, direct and goes right into the body and soul. As I have gone through practical situations I can feel much with my clients. And in addition to that what I appreciate most about horses is that they do not use the "conjunctive", the what if and could and would words. They prefer the "as is" status and they are far from storytelling.

*Case Example(s) with description of a typical human-horse interaction: Please give a description of why this interaction takes place, who is part of it, and to what purpose. If possible, pick a case example that shows the theoretical approach as well as the horses' function(s), as well as how you as facilitator/team partner intervene/react/facilitate. Description of how you ensure the horses' welfare and wellbeing before, during and after the human-horse interaction.*

I work with my own horses. Mixed herd: male, female; young, old; little, tall; Spanish, Shetland ponies. Just a bunch of horses. I live with them, I care for them myself. I can tell you from the poo how they are today.

Almost all my horses are rescued horses. I used to call them traumatized. Nowadays I changed my wording to calling them horses with a past.

While working with them I am very sensitive to their state of mind and carefully observe their behavior and reaction in the current situation. The benefit for the horses can be, as I have seen many times, that they also grow during this kind of work and healing takes place on their side, too.

I ask my horses who wants to volunteer to work. I create a safe environment by providing lots of open space, no halters, and few ground rules. I watch them carefully as soon as I start talking to my clients and we enter the energetic space of my herd. I watch every single move; whatever they do and show is a piece of information for me during the whole process. I also watch myself carefully to see when I interpret too much, when I project too much and so on. In combination with the clients' reactions, I try to get the full picture in order to move on step by step.

The level where I am working now is:

- To analyze the human status by asking for arousal level, body scan and listening to their stories

- To watch the herd, observe and feel

- To get in touch with the self and then to ask for permission from a distance.

- To check expectations and what is really wanted from the horses.

- To boundary dance – to watch how someone approaches a horse and to see how the horse reacts to the human person

- To reflect on 1:1 sessions and not always with direct horse contact

- To find the individual's space in the herd

So far, I experience a very deep level of intense work which is fast and respectful. Any further work has not been necessary yet – it is in my tool case but not needed.

*Examples:*

A friend of mine wanted to go to Denmark for a four-week apprenticeship and she wanted to take two of her horses with her. She asked me for advice about what to do with one of her horses as somebody told her he does not like trailers, and she wanted him to move in of his own free will.

That's impossible! No wild horse would walk into a trailer to go to a course!

So she is in charge; she wants it, and the horse has to follow her.

My answer was this: In this case – you are the leader and have to make it as safe and comfortable for him as possible and you must not have any doubts!

She changed her focus and intention and it was no problem.

Assuming that you are a responsible person making wise decisions, you have to take the lead and go ahead. It is the same with children – if you are convinced that something is right and good for you and the child, the child will follow you because he trusts you; no matter how crazy this might look like to the outside world!

*Examples:*

I have had a client on site with me for a week. We worked an hour per day. She was in her fifties, single, no children, good job and a lot of frustration, family clean-up to do and sadness.

Her arousal level was quite high.

We stopped at a bench in our garden near the horses' paddock. No horse there. Then we started talking about why she did not know where to go in her life, what she wanted to do next, where her energy goes... finally we came to the point where she opened up and said that she feels lonely. Mare number one came and lay down in front of us. Then the client came to the point that she still wanted to run away from certain feelings. A gelding came past the mare without chasing her and stopped in front of us and fell asleep. Then the client opened up and all the sadness about the loss of not being able to have children of her own in her life came up. Mare number two came and lined up right in front of us. The client looked at the horses, crying, feeling sorry for what happened and I asked her "what do you feel like doing right now" and she just wanted to sit down in the grass and to follow her impulse. Mare number two lay down in front of her – I hardly ever see her lying down. So I gave my client the space and time to cry and let go being in the herd and the herd held her in a peaceful atmosphere.

These are the magical moments the horses offer us!

Another client – female, 32 years old. Well educated, in a relationship, successful business woman, living on a farm which was used as a riding stable before and is empty now. She really missed horses at the time, felt empty and did not know what to do next in her life. Arousal level 8 "Not knowing what to do; what if this and that happens? Am I doing things right" and so on. All this was going on while we checked the arousal level and did the body scan.

Once I asked her to turn around and look at the horses, her arousal level went down to five, once she met the horses it went down to four. Her body actually knew and remembered what to do and did not listen to her tornado heads (tornado heads are the voices in your head that drive you nuts and let your thoughts run in circles in a destructive way). And the horses acted accordingly, said "Hi" and integrated her in the herd.

During a team workshop, I could see that one lady was overly nervous and excited. She dreamed of a white horse during the night – without knowing that I have one. She was tense and said her arousal level was up to seven. Once I asked her after the check up to turn around and look at my horses, she connected with my white gelding and her arousal level went up to ten and she felt like panicking. She could not go closer to the herd. She felt real fear in her body. The horses reacted to her and moved even further away and started to eat hay. This lasted during the whole session. After working with my client for a short time, her anxiety issue calmed down and she was able to release bits and pieces. The minute we finished the herd started to move, passed by and started grazing on the pasture. Their job was done.

WORKING WITH HORSES IS QUITE EASY:

- OPEN YOUR HEART
- PUT YOUR EGO ASIDE
- AND START TO LISTEN TO YOURSELF AND THE HORSES

**About the Author**

Eva Balzer has 12 years of consulting experience with large corporations. An avid student, she started studying alternative healing methods for animals in 2003 and has owned her own practice since 2009 (Herzensschule – School of the Heart). Her training includes studies in animal healing, TCM acupuncture, osteopathy, craniosacral work, animal communication, and energy and shamanic work, kinesiology, homeopathy and Reiki, coaching and consulting, and Gestalt systemic constellation work. Within the field of equine-facilitated learning, Eva has trained and mentored with Kathleen Barry Ingram (co-founder of the Eponaquest Approach) and trained in the HEAL method developed by Leigh Shambo in the USA. She also wrote a book on EFL for leadership. She lives with her family and a herd of 6 horses on an organic farm in lower Saxony, where she offers trainings and seminars.

CHAPTER 26

# Pepper – Project Trauma Support

Dr. Manuela Joannou

*I think I was born horse crazy.*

*This was odd because I lived in the city and no one I knew had any horses. None of my immediate relatives knew anything about horses either. I found out later that great-grandfathers on both sides were extreme horsemen. Who knows how these genetic things work?*

*I pestered and pestered my parents, letting them know how much I wanted to ride. All I wanted for my birthday and for Christmas each year was the chance to get on a horse.*

I had my first opportunity to go riding when I was 8 years old. I convinced my parents to let me catch a van that did the rounds of several shopping centers, picking up people and then taking them to the Circle J Ranch for the afternoon. I am very glad that my parents had no idea how dangerous horses could be or they probably would never have let me go. I had watched so many episodes of my favorite show Bonanza that I felt I intuitively knew how to ride. The first day at Circle J, I went out on a 2 hour trail ride, walked, trotted, cantered and then galloped back to the ranch on a stable-bound paint pony named Lucky. No riding instruction. No helmets. No fear.

My parents bought a farm when I was 10. We spent weekends and many deliciously long warm, hazy summers there while I was growing up. In the first week after we moved in, I had the entire neighborhood cased out and knew where all the horses were. Most were neglected ponies that were running with the cows in farmers' fields. They had been bought at a barn sale at one time or another for children or grandchildren who soon lost interest. The farmers were quite amused when this 10 year old city kid knocked on their door asking if she could work with their horses!

I had no tack, no saddles or bridles. A lead rope was a luxury. Usually a halter and a few pieces of bailer twine were all I had to work with. I was UNTRAINED!

But I had the luxury of endless time and unbridled (pardon the pun) enthusiasm. I would sit for hours on those long summer days, stroking, brushing, and talking to the horses, once I learned some ingenious tricks of how to catch the wild rascals.

Horses are naturally curious beings. They are suspicious of your intentions at first, but if you let them sniff you over (those first sniffs are often snorts) they soon come to realize you are not a threat, and that you may even provide some entertainment and the occasional treat. Soon the horses that initially ran away when approached were following me everywhere. They would race to the fence when I called them.

I always moved slowly but deliberately when working with the horses. Everything was gradual. First brush the neck. Then move to the head and around the ears, always keeping up a steady stream of conversation. You can tell those horses any childhood and teenaged secrets, did you know? They seem always interested and non-judgmental. They seem uncannily able to provide just the right encouragement and support at the sad parts.

After the horses' necks and heads were easily brushed, stroked and scratched/tickled, we would move on to the backs, girth area and belly and legs. The hind quarters, flanks and back legs could provide some excitement at times. The horses told you when you were pushing it and had gone too far: the ears flick back, the flanks tense up, the tail twitches. Sometimes the back leg comes up in a rather threatening manner. Time to go back to what you know has already been allowed. And then back to the forbidden areas again, in a matter-of-fact "so what's your problem with this?" sort of way. Finally, the horses give in and relax. It's almost as if they sigh and say, "what's the use of protesting?"

Their bodies totally yield. You can soon touch them everywhere. You learn the ticklish spots and the itchy spots. And soon they come to you, presenting their itches, trusting that you will scratch just the right way.

Trust and curiosity. If I had to pick the two characteristics of horses that allow major interaction with humans, those would be the two. Horses are prey animals. They are forever on guard, ready to flee, kick or rip their teeth into a real or perceived threat. They are also herd animals and learn to relax into letting other, more dominant beings lead and protect them. Humans can step into the role of leader, protector and, also, director, feeder, comfort provider and entertainer if they move in strategic and well thought out ways. The natural instincts of the horse, along with their innate curiosity and tendency to develop a pecking order, make them ideal partners for teaching and therapy. They must always remain on guard, intuitively assessing risk, threat and danger. Their lives depend on it in evolutionary terms. The social fabric of the herd dictates that horses must be experts in the fine nuances of who's who: which horses are the leaders, the directors, the protectors? Which are the annoying ones and those who garner little or no respect? Who are the young and vulnerable that can be foolish but need special consideration from their elders to survive?

Once the horses were used to being handled everywhere, it was no big deal to gradually slide over off the fence and onto their back. First a little pressure on their back from your leg. Then more. Then you gradually slide your leg over to the other side, hanging onto the fence so you can hop back if the horse explodes. They rarely do when you go gradually enough. The next thing you both know, you are on the horse's back. Things can get interesting here. Always slow, steady, reassuring movements and talking. Sometimes you get the sudden spark and then the bucking bronco ride. Once you pick yourself up off the ground it's back to the fence. Let's start over, more slowly, more gently.

Time is always the essential ingredient. Some things, with some horses, you just can't rush. Others buy into their compliance quite quickly.

When I was 16, a lady I knew asked me to take her 4 year old quarter horse/standard-bred to train him. His name was Pepper. She had bought him from the lady who bred him as a pet and he had never been worked. He had never been away from his mother. He didn't even lead that well.

I went over to get him to bring him to our farm early one day at the end of June, as soon as school was out for the summer. I had to lead him 5 km home and this was, as predicted, an interesting trip. He protested profusely at having to leave his mother. He bucked and reared and pulled and it was all I could do to hold him. His shrill whinnies were hard on the ears. We got about half way home and he had had enough. He planted his 4 feet firmly on the pavement in the middle of the road and refused to budge another inch. Exasperated and close to tears myself, I didn't know what to do. I worried about what would happen if a car came. I went as far ahead of him as the lead would allow and turned my back on him. I thought, "OK if that's what you want, we can stand here all day." After what seemed to be a very long time, I felt the rope go slack, and Pepper came up and stuck his nose in my back as if to say "so now what?"

We finally made it home, after about 4 hours. Ours was a long lane leading into the front yard of our farmhouse. Cars, bikes, barking dogs, and many children of various sizes engaged in various activities were what greeted poor Pepper when we arrived. He freaked, rearing up, pulling me off the ground and almost ripping my shoulder out of the socket. I will never forget how my 4 year old little sister came out of the house and stood on the front step, seeing a horse and clasping her hands with great glee. She was used to my bringing horses home and taking her for rides. "Can I ride him! Can I!?, Can I just have one little ride?" she pleaded as Pepper dragged me across the lawn with my boots leaving skid marks in the grass. But I was as persistent and as stubborn as that horse. Over the next few hours, after letting him get his nervous energy worked out by chasing the cows in the field (he had never before seen cows), I had the saddle on him, the bridle as well, and I rode him around the field at a walk, trot and canter. That day was a big day in Pepper's sheltered life. He fought, then yielded, then became curious, and then began to trust and follow.

The rest of the summer was a blur of long trail rides and hours of sitting in the pasture with Pepper. I would ride him everywhere; over fallen trees on the trail, into water, across scary, rickety (his perception) bridges, down into sand pits and up the other side. He never seemed to mind that we rarely saw other horses. He was content being with his human. He also bonded with my golden lab Sam, who was deeply offended if she ever saw me get the saddle out but was not invited on the ride.

At the beginning of August, the nearby town of Middleville hosted its annual Pioneer Day Festival. This was where all the farmers brought out their antique tractors and farm machinery with the steam engines and whistles. Thousands of people came from miles around. The highlight of the weekend was the parade. I rode Pepper proudly in the parade, with steam engines coughing, backfiring, sputtering, their shrill whistles blowing and with thousands of cheering people lining the narrow street. Pepper pranced proudly and excitedly along in the parade like he had done it every day of his life. I had only been riding him 6 weeks by that time, but he trusted me completely and I trusted him. I had learned that if he was nervous, I could reassure him with a confident demeanor and calming voice.

One day later on that summer, Pepper and I started out on an all-day trail ride. I had planned to find an old trail I had heard about that joined two township roads. I found the beginning of the trail at first, but after some time it petered out. Too many years and too many trees had obliterated the path. I soon found us trying to maneuver our way through increasingly thicker woods and brush. Finally, I had to get off Pepper's back because I couldn't fit under the branches anymore. I tried leading him for a while, but as it was getting dark, I had the scary realization that we were hopelessly lost. Finally, even Pepper had had enough and firmly planted his feet, refusing to go one step further. I was quite beside myself. I am sure Pepper was not used to seeing me so frazzled. Once again, I went to the ends of his reins, hoping he would give in and be willing to continue on. Eventually, he came up behind me and shoved me. He was ready to go. I had no clue as to which direction we should try, but started to head off in one direction. Pepper had a different idea. He quite insistently pushed me toward the stirrup. I was quite incredulous, but it certainly seemed like he wanted me to get back in the saddle. Totally resigned at this point, I climbed up on his back and gave him full slack in the reins. He promptly picked his way out of the bush, choosing a path that would not knock me off, and within an hour he had me back on the road we started on. Horses have great geographic and geometric instincts. We got home after dark, but I was extremely grateful to that horse.

Sadly, at the end of that summer when we moved back to the city, I had to give Pepper back. He ended up going to another farm. One day when the owner of the farm was away at work, some children visiting a neighbor went into the barn and did something to Pepper in his stall. No one quite knows what, but he was never the same again.

He became terrified of people, especially children. I never had the chance to work with him again, which has been a lifelong regret.

Trust is sacred. It is precious. Trust can take a long time to build, but it can be lost forever in the wink of an eye. Another life lesson our horses can reveal.

Horses have so much to teach us. A skilled therapist and a horse make a great therapeutic team.

- Horses teach patience.
- They teach you that ultimately, you are not in control.
- They teach you to respect the boundaries of other beings and let you know in no uncertain terms when you have crossed theirs.
- They teach you that gentle persuasion gets you much further than attempts to bully and control.
- They let you know if your demeanor, body language and tone of voice are threatening or menacing.
- They tell you when your lack of confidence is making your efforts inefficient and weak.

- They tell you that you need to back down on your pressure when you have been given compliance.

- They are the great levelers. It does not matter how much or how little power or status you have or how many stripes on your uniform, everyone is treated the same. Their curiosity makes them interested and attentive to you.

- They have an uncanny way of picking up on your emotions and responding to them.

- They prompt you to start considering just what resources are available to you to reach your goals.

- But most importantly, they teach you that commitment, loyalty, unconditional love and connection are the most powerful agents of healing and the most beautiful things in life.

Fast forward many years. I am now a family physician and an emergency physician with over 25 years experience. Like most people who work in emergency services, I have been involved in some very difficult cases. I have worked with many fine people who have also had many exposures to traumatic incidents. I've become conscious of the need to strengthen and to sustain our physical and psychological resources to be able keep doing this work.

As a family physician, I have always been interested in the human condition, and psychotherapy has been a large part of my practice. Over the years, I have become quite aware of the limitation of our approaches to psychotherapy, and the rather poor job we are doing with respect to mental health services in general.

We have increasingly limited financial and professional resources. An article in a Canadian medical publication recently was entitled "Our Shrinking Shrinks," referring to the fact that there are fewer physicians being trained in psychiatry and those who do practice this specialty are more likely to gravitate toward addressing the mental health concerns of the affluent "worried well".

There has been increasing discussion in the media about the problem of post-traumatic stress disorder in our military and first responder population. We have had many high-profile suicides and even murder-suicides committed by soldiers and police officers who were once considered heroes and warriors, but their subjection to various horrendous situations and circumstances left them fighting a most difficult enemy: the demons that took over their minds, bodies and souls. PTSD causes heart-wrenching wrecks of careers, family life and relationships, financial status, sense of identity and dreams of a fulfilling future.

In July 2014, one of the paramedics I had worked closely with and had known well for years ended his life by suicide. None of us working with him saw this coming. We were all devastated. He had a lovely young family and was a well-respected professional. This very tragic incident so close to home made me feel  strongly that something needed to be done to prevent more like it. I dove into learning as much as I could about Post Traumatic Stress Disorder and Operational Stress Injuries and especially how they affected our military and first responder communities.

I was fortunate to cross paths with many wonderful people who were working in the field, many of whom were true pioneers. I am grateful to many mentors who graciously took the time to answer my many questions and point me in the direction of more resources. I am also extremely grateful to the wonderful partners that have joined me in launching Project Trauma Support, a novel program addressing PTSD in first responders and military personnel in Canada.

It became apparent to me that although PTSD obviously affects the minds and wreaks havoc on the physiologic states of those afflicted with PTSD, the real entity that is so difficult to treat and is the most likely to drive a previously brave warrior to suicide is the moral injury. Moral injury is that complex conflict that arises within one's conscience and soul when incidents and circumstances transgress what we know to be right and just.

If you did something you know morally you should not have done, or you did not do something that you should have done, or you bore witness to something that was just plain wrong and were helpless to intervene, you are a candidate to develop moral injury. Sometimes you may have found yourself in a situation where there is just no right answer. You are damned if you do and damned if you don't. This can also cause moral injury; a compromise of moral and ethical standards. The symptoms of moral injury torture the soul. They include guilt, shame, horror, anger, and a pervasive sense of injustice. They lead to self-reproach, isolation, explosive and unpredictable behavior, and numbing, either psychologically or chemically, potentially leading to addictions. The degree of the moral injury depends on your upbringing, your own paradigms of how you fit into the world, and your past experiences. It has become quite apparent to our team that a person's individual moral injury often is uncannily linked to aspects of his previous life experiences which left him vulnerable or psychologically under-resourced and under-defended.

The current "evidence based" treatments for PTSD are cognitive processing and prolonged exposure. These are used extensively because they are what were originally studied by Veteran's Affairs in the U.S. Both of these approaches are time consuming and resource intensive and sadly do not show much clinical improvement, even in the extensive research that has been completed using these modalities.

Addressing thought processes has limited success because it is not the higher cognitive centers of the brain that drive the emotional and physical reactions that are the symptoms of PTSD. Recent neuroimaging studies have given us more accurate mapping of the various brain structures and their specific functions. These do not show us how to calm raging anger or paralyzing fears or to soothe an injured soul, however. We cannot just "talk our way out" of these.

Dr. Bessel Van Der Kolk's groundbreaking book *The Body Keeps the Score* very thoroughly describes why cognitive based approaches have limited effectiveness in the treatment of PTSD. The physiologic effects of PTSD are best addressed through body centered therapies and modalities: yoga, Tai Chi, physical exercise and massage, etc. The moral injury must be treated using specialized approaches.

We have found that moral injury can be healed by human connection. Those suffering from PTSD need support, understanding, unconditional positive regard, forgiveness, acceptance, and compassion. These are the only antidotes to shame, guilt, anger, fear, and sadness.

Throughout the history of mankind, the human condition has been forged with war and all its cruelties, untold hardships, and the fear that comes from instability and unpredictability. Ancient civilizations coped by sticking together and looking out for each other. Mythology is the collection of stories that tell the tales of human struggle and victory. Ceremony, symbols, traditions, and initiations were all used to acknowledge and honor warrior stories, tragedies, courage and vindication. Meditative practices were the link to the mysteries of nature, Mother Earth, abundance and peace.

Somehow, we have slid off this platform of contemplation and connection. We are isolated, paradoxically, in this world of social media. In the quest for personal achievement and ownership of material objects we have lost our communal spirit.

Because we have lost our tribe, there is no sense of belonging, security and unconditional acceptance. We have lost our belief that ultimately the world is a benevolent place. The moral injuries of the soul are only healed in love and connection.

Animals are creatures of nature. They are links to evolution and testaments to survival. Their instinctive behaviors demonstrate examples of the victory of vitality over adversity. Horses have a unique place in the history of mankind and the stories of mythology.

Horses went to war with humans. They were instrumental in travel and hunting for food. They participated in the work that was done to claim the soil and to build basic shelters and even entire civilizations.

It makes perfect sense to revisit the unique relationship between horses and humans when we try to help those individuals struggling with injuries that have ravaged their sense of security, worth and identity. The horses' natural willingness to engage, their curiosity and matter of fact relating to humans make them unique partners. Horses do not judge what you have done or seen in the past. They do not care about your accomplishments or status. They model perfectly the art of living mindfully, in the moment. They appraise everyone based on their current state and behavior. They give willingly once you demonstrate the art of kindness, gentleness and benevolent intent. They will soon demonstrate the repercussions of your anger, loss of patience or lack of concern for their comfort and wellbeing. They exemplify perfectly the art of learning and retaining important lessons without remaining in a high alert state once immediate danger has passed. We all know how horses will react when they return to a place where something spooked them years before. Yet once the dog who was chasing them around the paddock is locked up, they peacefully go right back to their grazing.

People who have been particularly traumatized by those they should ordinarily trust often have difficulty forming the trusting relationships with others that can help them heal. These people are often better off with equine "therapists", at least at first. It seems that transference issues are not transferable to four legged beings.

Herd behavior also models healthy communication, connection and community. The herd moves together and stays together. No one is left behind. If one member acts in an obnoxious or unacceptable way, he is quickly reprimanded (a well-placed kick or bite seems to work) and then everyone gets over it and it is business as usual. No grudges. No ongoing dramas. No sense of entitlement or righteousness.

There will always be leaders and dominant ones. In the wild, these stronger beings emerged as the protectors and guards. When they became old or injured, they graciously stepped down and let other emerging leaders take over, but they were still respected and maintained their importance and value in the herd. Horses in a herd feel safe because they all keep watch over each other and stay alert to signal any potential dangers. The focus is not on individual preservation but the wellbeing of all.

The success of our Project Trauma Support program is based on connection. We create a safe space to allow vulnerability to be exposed and gently addressed. The defenses used to cover up and protect pain and vulnerability are what create the symptoms of PTSD. These are the symptoms that are distressing to the individuals and their families. Non-judgmental, unconditional love and empathy from respected tribe/team members are the elements that heal wounds caused by trauma. We believe this is the only way.

In our Project Trauma Support retreats we utilize physical fitness training, meditation, adventure, music, art therapy, and reflective journeying to allow our participants to reprocess their experiences and create new narratives that allow them to let go of maladaptive defenses and coping mechanisms. Our equine partners are invaluable in our work.

Horses cannot be fooled. They do not fall for even carefully constructed defense mechanisms. They can and will, without apology, let you know exactly what they think of you and your approach. A skilled therapist will pick up on the subtler demonstrations of what the horse is sensing and point out the relevant messages.

For many, being in the presence of horses is exciting. For some, it is even scary. In either case, it jars participants out of the numb state that many with PTSD slide into as a coping mechanism. Addressing this fear offers an opportunity to examine and deal with fear in a situation where that fear may be appropriate (for those who have no prior experience with horses). So often people with PTSD deal with a pervasive hyper-vigilance and fear that is not called for by the situation. It is useful to compare and contrast these two types of fear that have similar symptoms.

Group exercises with the horses allow unique challenges that call for collective problem solving and teamwork reminiscent of training missions that build camaraderie. In summary, our equine partners have much to offer as we embark on our mission to help our injured first responders and military personnel recover from the wounds of their trauma. It is our experience at Project Trauma Support that the healing gifts offered by horses are transformative and give lasting benefits.

**About the Author**

Manuela Joannou M.D CCFP(EM) is the Medical Director and Founder of Project Trauma Support, in Perth, Ontario , Canada. She is a Family Physician and Emergency Physician with over 25 years' experience

CHAPTER 27

# The Role of the Horse

## The Therapeutic Philosophy of Horse Sense of the Carolinas, Inc.

Shannon Knapp

*Although Horse Sense of the Carolinas (Horse Sense for short) has offered predominantly EAGALA-based services from 2003-2010, and a predominantly Natural Lifemanship/Trauma-Focused Equine Assisted Psychotherapy approach since 2010, all the people and organizations with whom and under whom I have studied have taught me and have added something of how Horse Sense approaches EAP & EAL.*

Since 2010-2011, Horse Sense has evolved its offerings to include mounted work with clients in the form of limited Therapeutic Riding and Trauma-Focused Equine-Assisted Psychotherapy, which includes both riding and unmounted work. We have very specific and clear distinctions among the methodologies in our toolkit. We feel we can meet 75-85% of our clients' needs utilizing solely groundwork, *and* we have begun offering these other modalities to address the other 15-25% of needs we feel are best treated with some form of mounted work. Our overwhelming commitment is to the client, not to a specific methodology or model. That said, we strive to be "clean and clear" about what, how, and why we employ different modalities, and constantly to challenge ourselves and each other in this process to articulate the reasons that drive what we are doing. Below are some of the key ideas informing the Horse Sense overall philosophy, as they have crystallized for me throughout the years, followed by our approach to the unique role of the horse in EAP/EAL.

## 1.   Concept of What Promotes Change

Pain is a very strong motivator; with sufficient discomfort, one becomes open-minded enough to start seeking answers. Pain and discomfort are the walls most people run into before they become ready to change. My experience is that people create, cause, and seek out change in their life when they get into enough discomfort or recognize the ineffectiveness of the approach they have employed to create something different in their life. Without enough need to change, there is no motivation to do so or to follow through. As Stephanie Burns says, *"Learning isn't fun."* In my experience, neither is change.

## 2.   Process-Focused vs. Goal-Focused

In some definitions of EAP, "goal-focused" is part of the description. While I recognize that anytime actual therapy is taking place there are always treatment goals and hence there is an unavoidable trajectory toward the goals, the description of EAP as "goal-focused" causes me to flinch a bit. I am concerned that this description causes practitioners to think more about short-term solutions rather than long-term ones, and focuses too much on outcomes rather than the process. Goal-focused programming can create much benefit and relief temporarily, but does not produce the lasting change necessary for long-term recovery from ineffective and/or destructive behaviors.

I find that when an agenda is set more for what clients "should" or "need to" experience, or there is more attachment to how something should look, then less true learning actually happens. The efforts become (and are felt by the clients as), at best, forced and often condescending. I find the effects of being goal-driven and agenda-focused causes problems for horses as well.

## 3.   Learner-Centered, Experiential Approach

Part of what we strive for at Horse Sense is creating a learner-centered environment for the client. People learn more effectively as they find their own answers from within instead of seeking answers from the outside, from an "expert". The horse supports this learner-centered approach by providing clients with a means to see the response to their behavior, to change that behavior in real time, and to experiment with alternatives. As the website for the Association of Experiential Education (AEE) states: *"Experiences are structured to require the client to take initiative, make decisions, and be accountable for results. Throughout the experiential learning process, the client is actively engaged in posing questions, investigating, experimenting, being curious, solving problems, assuming responsibility, being creative, and constructing meaning"* (www.AEE.org)

This does not, however, mean that clients should be left to their own devices when the skill set they currently possess is clearly unequal to the task at hand, nor is a shrug an appropriate therapeutic intervention for the vast number of clients experiencing trauma that we have encountered here at Horse Sense. Trauma-informed care is often lost in rigid experiential approaches to the detriment of the client.

## 4.   Power Dynamics & Gurus

Through my personal experience, my background as a college teacher, and in my experience with other equine-assisted practice and training programs, I like how a team approach decentralizes power; no one person has "the right answer" from the traditional teaching paradigm. Whereas the normal classroom sets up the right and wrong answers as known a priori, the learner-centered model is open-ended; there is no right or wrong.

A treatment team also reduces the possibility of what I call the "Guru Effect," in which the therapist or facilitator is set up to be idealized, creating dependence rather than independence. This is certainly something I see a lot in the EAP/EAL field. I certainly also see the horses being identified as the "Gurus" as much as the facilitators are, something that is insulting to the horses even while it attempts to privilege them.

## 5.   Team Approach

In addition to de-centralizing power the two-person team model also brings two human sets of eyes to each client session, a dynamic I feel is critical. Each professional has a main area of focus, one on the client and much of the verbal communication, the other on the horse and the non-verbal communication. A single facilitator having to concentrate on everything often leaves room to miss nuances and details, which is often where the heart of the matter lies. As an Equine Specialist, I really appreciate the many layers of information coming from the horse's body language alone. The mental health professional, likewise, is deeply engaged with the client, the intellectual process of the client, and the level of understanding of the client. Further, the two-person team also presents an opportunity for modeling communication, interaction, and other key life-skills for clients. Also, in terms of safety and legality, I find multiple sets of eyes are preferable.

There is also what I call the "Shoulder-to-Shoulder" effect in the team approach. Instead of being in the front of the classroom or opposite the client, "squared off" opposite the client, the facilitators in Horse Sense EAP/EAL are more often "shoulder-to-shoulder" with the client, examining the situation and being curious and inquisitive about possible solutions alongside the client.

These are some of the driving ideas behind the practice of Equine Assisted Psychotherapy at Horse Sense. There are also some key ideas for us about the role of the horse in the process, outlined below.

## 6.  Value of and Purpose of the Horse

First, EAP and EAL practices offer a great opportunity for horses who do not fit in the traditional or normal horse world. It gives them a chance to grow, develop, thrive, and give back. Horse Sense began from a desire and a recognition of the need to re-home and place young, happy, healthy *unrideable* horses from a nearby horse rescue and rehab. These horses were considered "useless" and were very hard to place because of their physical limitations, and were languishing. So there is a huge world that has opened up for many such horses in EAP/EAL practices. This makes our program at Horse Sense, first and foremost, "good for both of us", not just for the humans (as so many therapeutic practices with horses privilege the client over the horse, to the detriment of both).

## 7.  The Role of the Horse in Equine-Assisted Psychotherapy

Although much is made (and should be made) of the role of humans – clients and facilitators – in the therapeutic process of equine-assisted psychotherapy (EAP), we must not forget that the horse is still the salient part of the puzzle, and our focus should be directed toward the vital role the horse plays and the unique gifts equines offer. To begin, let us look at how the role of the horse in an EAP session is not only significantly different than in a therapeutic riding session but also remarkably different from an equine-assisted learning (EAL) session.

In therapeutic riding or in hippotherapy, most of the time we want horses to respond in trained and specific ways, rather than to behave naturally, offering up their unique physical gifts: gait, movement, etc. To invite the horse to act like a prey animal while being ridden by therapeutic riding and hippotherapy clients is counter-productive to these goals. In EAL we are often in the process of teaching or moving towards some pre-determined goals and/or agenda, which necessitates some level of teaching and instruction about how to engage with horses towards those goals.

With that in mind, we often oblige the horse to behave in certain ways and not in others, depending on the goals set out for the session; whether it is learning and demonstrating respect for a behaviorally-challenged school group or increasing creativity and communication for a professional development group.

What is possible in EAP, however, is for *the whole horse to be invited to the party: mentally, emotionally, and physically*. That is the rich opportunity present in EAP, in which the horse brings the unique gift of feedback by offering a clean, clear response to the way humans "show up," or interact with the horse. This gives clients an opportunity to check, among other things, perceptions of themselves against the perception of others, in this case, the horse. How is the horse able to give this very valuable feedback? Because of evolution, the horse is especially fine-tuned in his ability to read others. Key components to the horses' development that cause them to be experts in feedback are laid out in Dr. Robert Miller's *Understanding the Ancient Secrets of the Horse's Mind*, one of the most important book on horse psychology for the field of EAP. These "secrets", or inherited behavioral traits, include: the instinct to flee, to be perceptive to danger, and to have a quick response time.

## 8.  The Instinct to Flee

The instinctual propensity of horses to flee when uncertain offers obvious visual feedback for people. (Bear in mind that a fleeing horse during a session does not necessarily indicate something negative in a person.) This instinct goes hand in hand with the next trait: being perceptive to danger. Horses are incredibly perceptive to the world around them, to "people, places, changes and things," as Pat Parelli would say. Horses can offer feedback about parts of ourselves that we, with our large neocortex, have rationalized away, ignored, or are just unable to see. The third trait – response time – amplifies the first, in that rarely is a fleeing horse slow or plodding but instead is usually responding swiftly.

## 9.  Opposition Reflex

Another critical element to the role of the horse in EAP is opposition reflex. Opposition reflex can be simply defined as a prey animal's automatic response to predator behavior: if the predator likes an idea or a course of action, it cannot be good for the prey, so opposing it is the safest course. It is in observing, understanding, and working with this trait in horses that much fertile therapeutic ground can be covered in EAP sessions.

This is particularly relevant when working with any teenager (the human embodiment of opposition reflex!). They, like horses, are engaged in important developmental work when exercising opposition reflex in relation to the adults and others in their world.

Also, significant in this regard are youth with Oppositional Defiant Disorder (ODD) and Conduct Disorder (CD). However, one does not have to work with youth in order for this to be a significant part of the EAP process. A psychotherapist's client load is full of examples of adults who engage in behavior that actively pushes away, almost as instinctual behavior, the very thing(s) which they desire, to their detriment. Working with horses can give these clients the opportunity to experience how their own opposition reflex operates. However, a horse or a client left in the brain state from which that opposition reflex stems (the survival part of the brain), is by no means the goal here at Horse Sense. I have spoken to other "professionals" in the field who *love* their untouchable, uncatchable, wild horses, specifically and deliberately encouraging that behavior as an ongoing state, as it serves them in their agenda with their clients. This is akin to deliberately withholding treatment from clients.

## 10.  Clean Listening: A Different Agenda

Another very significant element the horse brings to EAP is what I call "clean listening" (with a nod to David Grove's "Clean Language"). Because horses disregard or simply do not register or care about all the distractions which often make up human communication (what kind of car you drive, what kind of tennis shoes you wear, how your hair is cut, etc.), horses actually listen to us at a much different and deeper level to the point where they "attune" to us. Attunement, as Daniel Goleman describes in his book *Social Intelligence*, is *"listening with full receptivity,"* which horses do so well, without much of the baggage that humans bring. This can be an incredible gift to humans who either never had or can no longer rely on familiar, and often dysfunctional, ways of relating but must explore more unfamiliar, and often more anxiety-provoking but growth-promoting, ways to connect.

Of equal importance to what the horse does bring to session is what the horse does not. Although many people speak of the horse being a clean slate, as having no agenda, that is not true in the strictest sense. Of course, horses have an agenda that is present all the time: survival. Their hierarchy of needs is most simply broken down as safety first (survival), comfort next, then play or food, depending on the horse. To deny the horse's agenda for survival is counterproductive in a therapeutic environment.

## 11. More than a Mirror

As we sort out the various ways we talk about our work in our field, I want to invite others to consider "attunement" as opposed to "mirroring". Attunement, to me, is a much richer and deeper concept than mirroring. Our field often uses the term "mirroring" to describe what the horse does in client sessions, but I think the process is different than simply "reflecting". When I think of reflection, I think of the mirror, in this case the horse, being subsumed to the process. But the horse does not disappear in relationship with us in EAP/EAL; the horse obviously continues to exist.

What does happen more closely resembles a deep, instinctual listening of the horse to the emotional state and the body language of the client, the same kind of deep presence horses seem to exhibit in most moments of their lives. The word attunement rings truer to me in describing this process than mirroring.

## 12.  Facilitator and Client Engagement: 3D vs 2D

Of interest also is how facilitators engage with horses during EAP sessions. Any facilitator is at his or her best when responding to the needs of the client(s) and the horse(s) in any given moment foremost, rather than being beholden to theoretical or methodological approaches. Facilitators at Horse Sense move in and out of being 3D and being 2D with clients and horses. Briefly, 3D contact happens in the check-in, closing, and processing portions of a given session and is the most likely time to see facilitators in a small circle with the client or with any one of the people involved in the session, perhaps petting a horse who has walked in to join that circle. What I call 2D contact involves getting out of the way (literally and figuratively) and allowing the client and the horse to connect, to engage and to process, unhindered by the facilitators. Although always mindful of the needs of clients and horses, including needs for safety and a safe place to learn and practice new behaviors, facilitators at Horse Sense operate best when they are focused on allowing the relationship between client and horse(s) to develop naturally, even if the patterns are unhealthy ones. We need first to "see" the problem(s) together before we can do anything about it; both with horses and humans.

This leads to a brief overview of both the conscious and unconscious ways clients engage with horses in session. The conscious ways most often discussed include:

- live problem-solving or learning and practicing new behaviors in a natural setting "in vivo", in the moment

- learning and building co-regulation of senses and emotions with the horse in order to learn self-regulation

- opportunities for feedback, as discussed earlier.

Co- and self-regulation, specifically as it relates to trauma, may not always be the presenting problem, but the overwhelming preponderance of Horse Sense clients have experienced some degree of trauma, hence our pivot towards a more trauma-informed approach to EAP/EAL, and our deeper dive into the physiological impact of the work we are doing.

## 13.  Use & Tool Debate

There is much discussion (and wringing of hands) around the term "use" to describe the horse's role in equine-assisted sessions, as in "we use horses to teach people about themselves". I agree the term "use" can suggest domination and objectification, an attitude of viewing the horse as a prop or a tool for our purposes. No doubt, the term can diminish the importance of the horse's role and gifts in the process. In my experience, not everyone who uses the term "use" is evil or has a patent disregard for the value of the horse as a partner in the therapeutic process. (Interestingly, we are often trying to help clients recognize how they may better "use" their resources.) Many people I know who use the word "use" are incredibly respectful of horses and the gifts they bring to session. I have also seen the opposite, in which many who lean towards the "sentient being" language demonstrate incredible disregard for the well-being of the horse, "using" the horse more blatantly than those they see as their opposite.

There are mental health professionals who have deliberately chosen working with horses, as opposed to sand tray therapy, for example, as a means to help the client. So, in the strictest sense of the word, they are, in fact, using horses as an intervention. As a professional, I can see how the term "use" crops up in our conversations: horses are one method; they are not the only method to help people learn and change. However, at Horse Sense we encourage a reframe of language around the idea of using horses to *working* with horses, or *playing* with horses. As a recovering college English professor, words and word choice *do matter*, just as we regularly encourage reframing our language in lots of other ways.

When I think of the word "tool", which is another term that is often brought up to point out the objectification of the horse in some EAP/EAL practices, I again understand the sentiment behind the objection without assuming those who refer to the horse as a "tool" are bad. The phrase *"make me an instrument of thy peace"* comes to mind when I argue with myself (and I do!) about the term "use" and "tool". What is an instrument if not a tool? Ultimately, though, I am more interested in how I and others *treat and engage* with horses than in how we *speak about* horses. As Kris Batchelor, a respected colleague at Triple Play Farms outside Charlotte, NC, stated: *"I would challenge all of us to employ the same mindfulness around language that we use within sessions"* to this issue, observing that *"choice of language isn't always indicative of attitude"* (Personal communication, February, 2013).

## 14. Horses & What's in it for Them?

Other theoretical questions concerning the horse and his/her role in session are raised: What, if anything, is in it for the horse? Does there need to be some purpose for the horse as well as for the human? Assuming these same horses are getting their basic needs met by their barn, equine-assisted work is not a particularly taxing job for a healthy horse, although there can be instances in which burn-out, boredom, mental pressure, and anxiety can arise (see *More than a Mirror* for a deeper discussion on the impact of EAP/EAL on the horse, and various perspectives from the field on the subject).

At one point when I was on various committees for PATH International relating to the horse, the idea was suggested that equine-assisted practices should be mutually beneficial for both the horse and the human – horses *should* get as much out of the session work as the humans. I would posit instead that horses *can* get as much out of session work if practiced ethically and responsibly; if it is not good for both of us, eventually it is not good for either of us. If in EAP we behave in ways counter to this, we actually end up doing harm to our clients by perpetuating cycles of use and abuse, and objectification of others for our own ends, whether horses or humans.

I cannot say that I know many horses who would not rather be quietly grazing in the pasture instead of in a session with a client. But I also cannot say that most people wanting improvement and change in their lives do not initially balk at the work necessary to do so, trying to avoid the effort. Growth and development and change are not fun, for anyone. It can be difficult and messy and uncomfortable. The key difference between clients and horses (at least in some cases), is agency: humans can actively choose to seek a different solution (although many many more are court-ordered or otherwise coerced into treatment of various kinds). Horses, on the other hand, do not "get to choose" to go into treatment. They either end up at a farm where their ability to grow and develop their brains beyond survival mode is recognized, supported and encouraged, or they do not. What I do know and have seen through several thousand hours of client contact with the same four horses I started with in 2001: – some horses will thrive on this kind of work, and others will not enjoy it. We need to be aware of that and the impact of this on our clients and our horses.

## 15. Summary

EAP is such a powerful field for further exploration, as well as personal growth, because it is so rich in both "feel", both sensory and emotionally, during a session and in anything we do with horses, and in thought, before and after a session. It is this integration of thought, feeling and the senses that makes EAP such a robust treatment opportunity; able to make *the* difference for so many people. I am grateful and honored to have worked with the horses, clients, and other professionals I have encountered, and look forward to continuing to challenge myself and others to grow.

### About the Author

Shannon Knapp, M.A., is founder and president of both Horse Sense of the Carolinas, Inc., an internationally-recognized leader in the field of Equine Assisted Psychotherapy and Learning, and Executive Director of Heart of Horse Sense, a nonprofit dedicated to supporting free, professional Equine Assisted Therapy and Learning for Veterans and At-Risk Youth in Western North Carolina. Shannon has also published many books and curricula in the field of EAP/EAL, including *More Than a Mirror: Horses, Humans and Therapeutic Practices* and *Horse Sense Business Sense*, a primer in the business side of EAP/EAL practice. Shannon is a trainer for Trauma-Focused Equine Assisted Psychotherapy, is EAGALA Advanced Certified, and is Associate Faculty for Prescott College's Equine Assisted Learning Masters Concentration program. A professional in EAP/EAL since in 2001, she has more than 15,000 hours of client contact in EAP/EAL with a diverse range of diagnoses.

CHAPTER 28

# Natural Lifemanship's Trauma-Focused Equine Assisted Psychotherapy (TF-EAP)

## The Connected Relationship is the Vehicle for Change for Human and for Horse

Laura McFarland, PhD, Bettina Shultz-Jobe, MA, LPC, and Tim Jobe, BS

*Natural Lifemanship™, founded by Tim Jobe and Bettina Shultz-Jobe, is a process for building connected relationships based on principles derived from horse and human neuropsychology. The keystone of Natural Lifemanship is Trauma-Focused Equine Assisted Psychotherapy (TF-EAP). In this model of equine assisted psychotherapy (EAP) the relationship is the vehicle for change and the equine always participates as an authentic relationship partner and never as a tool, an object or a metaphor in the therapy process. Both mounted work and groundwork are important to this model and serve specific therapeutic purposes; however, regardless of the type of interaction and whether it occurs on the ground or while mounted, the cultivation of a connection within the relationship is always the central concern.*

Natural Lifemanship (NL) operates from the premise that if *a relationship is not good for both partners, it eventually is not good for either.* Another way of putting this is that for a relationship to be the vehicle of (positive, beneficial, transformative) change and healing for the human, it must actually be so for the horse as well. This is not mere ideology but is held as a truism. However, to appreciate this truism it is necessary to understand something of the history of the model, how the co-founders developed it, and its theoretical basis in neurobiology and trauma-informed care.

The purpose of this article is to describe how Natural Lifemanship conceptualizes the role of the horse in our TF-EAP model. To accomplish this, it is necessary to describe the model itself in some detail. The relationship between client and horse is so central to our model that it is impossible to talk about one without addressing all three (the horse, the client, and the relationship itself). So while we attempt to focus primarily on how the horse is conceptualized and how she participates in and benefits from TF-EAP, we will spend considerable time familiarizing the reader with the therapy model itself, which is oriented toward the healing of trauma in humans.

We acknowledge that there are many kinds of equine assisted practices that may deliver mental health benefits although they are not psychotherapy. By way of clarification, TF-EAP is indeed a psychotherapy model. As such, TF-EAP *must* be practiced by a *licensed mental health professional*, one who is qualified and meets all requirements established by the governing bodies wherever he or she practices. In addition to this licensure, practitioners of TF-EAP must be trained in Natural Lifemanship, which minimally requires a three-day live training course. TF-EAP also requires the presence of an equine professional (EP) trained in our approach. A mental health professional may serve in both roles if they have sufficient equine knowledge, skills and experience. We believe there are therapeutic benefits when qualified therapists and EPs co-facil-itate sessions, and encourage practitioners to work in teams when possible. We also recognize that there are times, when doing trauma work, that it is not appropriate for the client to have an audience. During these times, a dually trained therapist can more adequately meet the therapeutic needs of their client.

This paper is organized in two parts. In Part I, we provide an overview of the model and its theoretical foundations. In Part II, we examine key NL principles and their implica-tions for how horses participate in and experience TF-EAP. Specifically, we discuss why, if the relationship is the vehicle for change, it must be a real and not a metaphorical relationship. Additionally we consider why connection is always the goal, and why we say, "if it is not good for both, it eventually is not good for either". Furthermore, we clarify the distinction between compliance and cooperation from a neurobiological perspective and why the Principle of Choice is so critical to building a relationship characterized by cooperation. We share how pressure and release are used to build a connected and cooperative relationship. Finally, we discuss how every principle applies equally whether on the ground or while mounted, and we consider the implications of how the relationship between human and horse is conceptualized, especially during mounted work.

Throughout the paper we will draw connections between the empirical foundations of the model rooted in trauma-informed neuroscience (presented in Part I) and the principles that guide the entirely relational process of TF-EAP, including its ground and mounted component. In this way we explore the beneficial impact of this process on the neurobiology of the horse and the interpersonal neurobiology at play in the relationship between horse and human.

# Part I:

# The Neurobiology of Trauma and the Healing of Trauma through Natural Lifemanship

## 1.  A Brief History of the Model

Natural Lifemanship took root organically during a period in which co-founders Tim Jobe and Bettina Shultz-Jobe, together with their equine partners, were facilitating healing and healthy development for people of all ages, many of them youth, whose distresses could be traced to various kinds of trauma. Reflective of its co-founders, the model importantly emerges from two distinct yet complementary sets of expertise: the expertise of Tim, a horse trainer who has worked extensively with humans, and that of Bettina, a mental-health therapist who has worked extensively treating trauma-related mental health conditions, both with and without the help of horses.

Before Tim ever encountered the field now known as trauma-informed care, he observed the at-risk youth he worked with begin to flourish in their relationships with him and his horses, and yet continue to struggle in their relationships with other humans in their homes, school and community. Simultaneously he recognized that although they were able to befriend his horses, those same youth were unable to successfully ride the world-class quarter horses that he had trained in traditional ways. These observations led to the realization that if their relationships with horses were really going to help these youngsters in their daily lives, there would need to be some transfer of skills and of the qualities inside of them that seemed to emerge in the company of horses. At the same time, he recognized a need to refine his way of training horses so that a horse's response to a request made by a human handler was not dependent on the human's ability to control the horse's feet, which these youths were unable to do.

As an experiment Tim broke bonds with tradition. He started routinely asking himself whether his methods, and more importantly the intentions underlying his methods, were consistent with human psychology and the relationship principles that characterized healthy human relationships. This exercise resulted in subtle changes in the ways he would work with a horse. He considered, for example, that healthy human relationships are characterized by freely chosen reciprocity. Most parents of teenagers would agree that while they *naturally* (by virtue of being parents and protectors) hold the authority to establish all the rules of the relationship, they desire a relationship where it is not necessary to exercise such authority. A satisfying relationship between humans is one in which each party chooses to do what is right for the relationship; for example, cooperate with a request because it is the right thing to do – and not because they fear the consequences of not complying or because they seek an extrinsic reward for their compliance. Parents and teachers alike aim to help children develop the ability and tendency to freely make good choices, considering the well-being of others and their relationships in the choices that they make. In other words, we aim to help youngsters develop the capacity for "we" thinking instead of just "me" thinking, and healthy human psychology and relationships rest on this capacity for "we" thinking.

Tim realized that horses were capable of "we" thinking as well, but that exercising that capacity is roundly neglected by traditional horse training approaches that instead seek to establish a dynamic whereby the horse allows the human to think for him. In some ways, the struggles the youngsters exhibited in their human relationships could be traced back to parenting styles that sought to establish a similar dynamic – one in which the child unquestioningly complies and the adult assumes absolute authority for decision making in the relationship. The result may be an obedient child or a rebellious child, and one who enters adulthood having little to no experience freely making choices that exercise any level of "we" thinking. Natural Lifemanship began with the intention to help humans and horses mutually develop their innate capacity for "we" thinking through the process of building a connected and attuned relationship with each other, and for each to continue to exercise and further develop that capacity in all of their natural relationships.

Tim worked with a number of therapists co-facilitating EAP sessions based on this intention. Natural Lifemanship began to truly coalesce, however, when Bettina Shultz joined in the work, bringing with her a lens that had sufficient acuity to explain why the experiment seemed to be working and how it was contributing to humans and to horses reaching their respective potentials. The lens was that of Trauma-Informed Care.

## 2.  Trauma-Informed Care and Natural Lifemanship

Trauma-Informed Care (TIC) is an umbrella term used to describe a way of approaching the care and treatment of individuals, families, and communities affected by trauma. The foundation of this approach is an understanding of and respect for human neurobiology and neurodevelopment, specifically the ways that brain-body physiology develops, adapts and changes to accommodate experiences of acute or chronic traumatic stress. Natural Lifemanship's TF-EAP is a treatment approach that falls under this umbrella. We maintain that the relational process of TF-EAP beneficially reorganizes the neurobiology of both human and horse participants. It is important to note that TIC is not a specific treatment, nor is it limited to a specific mental health diagnosis such as PTSD. Rather, it is more like a lens or a framework that encourages one to *respect* (literally, *to look again* or to look beyond the surface) and consider what a person or animal has suffered and how individual experiences have shaped and modified the bodies, minds, and hearts in ways that have enabled them to cope and survive. This lens also brings into focus the likely origins of maladaptive emotional, behavioral and cognitive patterns that bring clients into the therapist's office to begin with. It changes our modes of inquiry as therapists. The question "what's wrong with you?" or "what is your diagnosis?" now becomes, "what has happened to you?" "What adaptations have occurred in your brain to accommodate the trauma you've experienced?" Adaptive behaviors are understood as protective so long as traumatic stressors are present. They become problematic, or maladaptive, when, as trauma expert, Dr. Bruce D. Perry puts it, "states become traits." (Perry, Pollard, Blakley, Baker & Vigilante, 1995).

The effective treatment of trauma leverages the brain's adaptive functioning through neuroplasticity. If a brain is able to organize itself to accommodate threat, it is able to re-adapt, or reorganize, to function in a world that is safe. The important question then becomes how does the brain become organized in the context of healthy development and how can its reorganization following trauma best be facilitated? Natural Lifemanship draws heavily on the work of leading experts in the neurosciences to answer this question. We equip mental health and equine professionals with the knowledge needed to most effectively partner horses and humans, helping each recover from trauma and develop the neurobiological capacity to self regulate and to make choices about how to behave in the context of relationships.

## 3.  Basic Brain Development of Humans and Horses

To understand and to practice TF-EAP effectively it is necessary to have an understanding of how the brain develops, how trauma impacts that development, and what kinds of interventions are effective in trauma recovery. This knowledge is necessary to understand fully how the horse facilitates healing in TF-EAP and therefore how we conceptualize his role, and why we believe the process returns similar benefits to the horse. We therefore provide a very brief overview of what we routinely teach students of Natural Lifemanship about the brain development of humans and horses.

As the hub of the vertebrate nervous system, the brain is responsible for the physiological development and maintenance of the entire physical organism, including, but not limited to, its mental activity and behaviors. The brain is complex and we do not attempt to be exhaustive when explaining its development. We find, however, that a basic foundation in neurodevelopment organized by its big ideas or overarching themes is most helpful in understanding how and why we conduct TF-EAP. When teaching the fundamentals of our model, we rely heavily on the work of neuropsychiatrist and child trauma expert Dr. Bruce D. Perry, who has developed a parsimonious model that breaks the complex processes of neurodevelopment into a set of core principles. These core principles then inform the ways we understand and treat children and adults impacted by trauma.

The Neurosequential Model of Therapeutics (NMT) (see Perry, 2001, 2002, 2006, 2008, 2009) is not a specific intervention, but rather a problem-solving approach to guide assessment and treatment. It is an approach to mental health treatment that is informed by neuroscience. The NMT is a key heuristic through which we assess client needs to inform the sequence and progression of treatment in TF-EAP; for example, when and in what ways mounted work is used. It also helps to inform how and when we use a specific intervention or technique from other therapeutic modalities like body-based therapies, or any of the cognitive or experiential therapies that may be employed in the context of or in conjunction with TF-EAP. We find that many different modalities can be employed within TF-EAP. Equally important to the Neurosequential Model is the process of building a connected relationship between human and horse; this is informed through the heuristic of the Natural Lifemanship principles, which are discussed in the next section. To appreciate the significance of the NL principles, however, it is necessary to begin with an understanding of the neurosequential principles of brain development.

Although Dr. Perry's Neurosequential Model focuses on developmental processes emphasizing early childhood experiences, it is a highly relevant approach to trauma treatment for people of all ages. It helps practitioners identify core developmental strengths as well as gaps that influence how an individual will experience and respond to trauma at any life stage. Positive developmental experiences result in greater resilience to traumatic insults later in the lifespan, while adverse experiences contribute to greater vulnerability and risk. Therefore, even when treating adults, the Neurosequential Model dictates that developmental experiences matter and should be considered when designing treatment plans. Professional TF-EAP practitioners work extensively with adults as well as with children and youth. Natural Lifemanship actively trains and certifies mental health professionals and EPs who work with veterans, people struggling with substance use and addictions, including eating disorders, and survivors of sexual violence, trafficking and political asylum, to name a few.

## 4.  Core Principles of Neurodevelopment

Firstly, it is worth noting that the context for human neurodevelopment is multidimensional and the process itself complex. Human development can be examined on many levels, from the microbiological to the cognitive to the psychosocial and even the collective. Whether we are concerned with neurons and synapses or familial bonding or cultural evolution, parallel processes are at play. There are certain universals that occur at all levels. These include growth, interaction, connection, and organization. Organization may be seen as the product of development while cellular growth, migration, connections and differentiation are its raw materials. With more than 100 billion nerve cells and quadrillions of interconnections between them, making any practical sense of developmental processes requires a macro perspective, allowing us to understand the broader principles of neurodevelopment in light of its key components.

**Neurodevelopment Principles According to the Neurosequential Model**
(see Perry, 2009).

**Principle 1: The brain develops in a sequential fashion from the bottom to the top, the inner to the outer, and from the least to the most complex.**

*"Simply put, the organization of higher parts of the brain depends upon input from the lower parts of the brain. If the patterns or incoming neural activity in these monoamine systems is regulated, synchronous, patterned, and of "normal" intensity, the higher areas will organize in healthier ways; if the patterns are extreme, dysregulated, and asynchronous, the higher areas will organize to reflect these abnormal patterns."* (Perry, 2009, p. 242)

**Main points**

- If one were to take a cross-section of the human brain and organize it according to the regions that are most responsible for mediating distinct functions, these would include the brainstem, diencephalon/cerebellum, limbic system, and cortex, which includes the neocortex (most newly evolved and outermost part of the brain). The prefrontal cortex is located in the prefrontal lobe, one of four lobes comprising the neocortex. As the brain organizes through the course of human development, it organizes sequentially in this order. In this way, brain development proceeds from the bottom to the top, the inside out, and from the primitive to the most complex throughout the course of development.

- Each major region develops and becomes organized and fully functional at different times during the developmental period (beginning inside the womb and continuing through the mid to late twenties and beyond). These specific times are critical periods during which qualities of experiences, both positive and negative, are especially formative.

- The entire brain and its regions are interconnected. Therefore the organization and functioning of any region depends on the organization and functioning of the region(s) that developed before it. Disorder and dysfunction of the more primitive regions cascade throughout the brain impacting the development of the higher regions.

### Clinical implications

- We must work to repair and reorganize the brain from the bottom up. Many traditional psychotherapy approaches aim to heal psychopathology from the top-down, through cognitive therapy. Complex trauma (such as drug or alcohol exposure in the womb, childhood abuse or neglect, relational loss or exposure to violence and chaos) occurs at the earlier stages of development and thus directly impacts the functioning of the areas of the brain that are developmentally active at that time, setting into motion a ripple effect that disrupts normal development from that point forward. Thus trauma-informed treatment must work to first reorganize the areas of the brain that were most sensitive at the onset of trauma. When treating those who have experienced trauma in adulthood, such as combat, violence, and rape, it is important to consider the individual's developmental history. By doing so one may identify sources of resilience and also vulnerabilities to trauma-related disorders and these will inform trauma treatment using TF-EAP.

### Principle 2: The brain organizes itself through activity, or interaction, and is modified through use.

*"The principle of use dependence is at the heart of effective therapy. Therapy seeks to change the brain. Any efforts to change the brain or systems in the brain must provide experiences that can create patterned, repetitive activation in the neural systems that mediate the function/dysfunction that is the target of therapy."* (Perry, 2009, p. 244).

### Main points

- The connections that organize the brain result from patterns of use and activation. The same principles apply to reorganizing the brain. It must be activated through use in patterned, repetitive ways. Where patterns of activation are highly rhythmic and thus predictable, myelination of pathways results in the efficient flow of information throughout the brain and nervous system.

## Clinical implications

- Rhythm and repetition are necessary for organization of any of the brain's regions. When attempting to reorganize the brain from the bottom up, we need to provide experiences that activate the target regions in rhythmic, patterned, repetitive ways. Each region of the brain is used for different purposes; so in order to activate a region responsible for mediating different functions, we must provide experiences that require its use. The brainstem, for example, regulates the senses, among other functions. Sensory input activates the brainstem. To heal and reorganize the brainstem, we must provide rhythmic, patterned, repetitive qualities of sensory input, which includes auditory and visual input, and even the experience of motion (such as rocking) that do not require the client's effort.

## Principle 3: Early childhood experiences matter most.

*"The simple and unavoidable conclusion of these neurodevelopmental principles is that the organizing, sensitive brain of an infant or young child is more malleable to experience than a mature brain. While experience may alter the behavior of an adult, experience literally provides the organizing framework for an infant and child. Because the brain is most plastic (receptive to environmental input) in early childhood, the child is most vulnerable to variance of experience during this time."* (Perry, 2009, p. 245)

## Main points

- The timing of developmental experiences has a profound impact. The same experiences will impact an individual very differently depending on the ages and stages of development during which the experiences occurred. This is because there are periods of development that are more sensitive than others and because development by nature is sequential and cascading. Individuals who have experienced trauma earlier in their lives or gestation are sensitized by that exposure and thus more vulnerable to future traumatic insults, even as adults. On the other hand, those whose early development was characterized by nurture, safety, and predictability develop greater resilience to future insults.

### Clinical implications

- To understand the impact of trauma on any one individual, it is necessary to know when the trauma(s) occurred and what qualities characterized the developmental trajectory during and up until those events.

### Principle 4: Relationships mediate all major developmental experiences

*"one recurring observation about resilience and coping with trauma is the power of healthy relationships to protect from and heal following stress, distress, and trauma. This relational modulation of stress is mediated by two interrelated and broadly distributed systems in the human brain: the stress response systems and neural networks involved in bonding, attachment, social communication, and affiliation."* (Perry, 2009, p. 246)

### Main points

- Because our species' survival has depended on it, we have evolved to seek safety in relationships. Our stress response systems ensure we react and respond to threat and stress in ways that keep us safe, and these are biologically interdependent with the neural networks that comprise our attachment and bonding behaviors.

### Clinical implications

- Healthy relationships are protective against toxic stress and allow for the restoration of the stress response system to a calm state following intense activation. There are two profound implications: 1) without positive relationships to modulate the activation of the stress response system, the chronically active state will eventually become a trait; and 2) the capacity to benefit from relational modulation, or co-regulation, is itself a product of early developmental experiences of bonding between infant and caregiver.

- It is often the case with survivors of complex trauma that this relational mediation is absent or severely compromised because early relationships were often not experienced as nurturing or safe. In these cases the capacity to benefit from positive relational interactions must be developed through rhythmic, patterned and repetitive (e.g., predictable and frequent) positive relational interactions. As this capacity develops, attuned relationships serve to co-regulate, allowing the individual's stress response system to shift fluidly between stress response states. This is the hallmark of self-regulation.

- Both the capacity for healthy relationships and the repeated experience of attuned relational interactions are critical to reorganizing the brain, which must occur before the individual who has experienced complex trauma is able to benefit from strictly cognitive-focused therapy.

- Therefore, for those of any age who present with attachment wounds, gaining the ability to create and to benefit from healthy relationships is critical to healing and should become a primary focus of therapy. It is for this reason that in trauma-focused therapies such as TF-EAP™, *the relationship is the vehicle for change.*

## 5. The Horse Brain and the Human Brain

### How the relationship enhances each

Horses and humans, as mammals, share a similar brain anatomy at the lower levels. Both species have a brainstem and cerebellum responsible for integrating sensory awareness with movement, such that the flight response is well attuned to the threat of predators (much more so in horses than humans). Both species also have relational drives that are interdependent with the stress response system. Horses find safety in their herds while humans are meant to find safety in their clans. Both are most vulnerable and experience heightened stress when isolated and unable to connect with those near to them. Because connection is so important to our survival, our brain chemistry predisposes us to seek connection through releasing rewarding neurotransmitters such as oxytocin and dopamine when we experience positive relational interactions. Simply put, when developmental experiences are optimal, connected relationships feel good to horses as well as to humans. The release of rewarding neurotransmitters such as dopamine results in learning as we come to associate our behaviors and other conditions with the flood of well being experienced when these neurotransmitters are released. The science of behavior modification seeks to manipulate the brain's natural responses to reinforce and thus shape desired behaviors while extinguishing others.

Humans who have experienced complex, relational trauma may not experience relationships as rewarding or calming. In fact, complex trauma wires the nervous system to be sensitized to close relationships as sources of threat, not comfort. For these clients, especially, relational therapy with horses is extremely effective. Horses provide a sort of carte blanche. They do not evoke the defense mechanisms (at least not immediately) that interfere with connection. A partnership with a horse is a safe place to experience vulnerability in relationship when human relationships are triggering. The relationship with the horse serves as a scaffold that allows the client to practice the skills needed in relationship and that enable them to begin to experience relationships as rewarding. The psychotherapy is the transfer of these skills from the horse-human relationship to human relationships.

While horses and humans share similar brain architecture, the distribution and concentration of neuronal cells and networks differ in each species. As prey animals, horses have well developed lower regions, resulting in finely tuned sensory perception that is highly sensitive to predators as well as well-coordinated, fluid bodily movement allowing for effective flight responses when they sense danger. With humans they share relational mid brain regions that allow for social bonding. Horses possess a neocortex with a primitive frontal lobe that is involved in attention and learning, although with repetition, motor habits are mastered and become increasingly efficient and automatic, resulting in less frontal lobe involvement. Like human youngsters, foals have a very short attention span that increases as the brain develops; and like humans, the ability to predict the dopamine release that comes with positive experience is central to learning. Finally, like humans, *horses don't discriminate between good and bad learning. They will search for the dopamine release regardless of how humans interpret their actions.* (Black & Peters, 2012).

This is why Natural Lifemanship believes that the principles through which we interpret and respond to both horse and human behavior in the context of the relationship are critically important. When we are in a relationship, whether we are aware of it or not, we are both teaching and learning how to be in a relationship, for better or worse. If a relationship is experienced as aversive or disconnected and lacking in care and nurturing, the dopamine release will occur in the context of avoiding the relationship or disconnecting and dissociating from it if physical avoidance is impossible. On the contrary, if a relationship is experienced as nurturing, attuned, safe and predictable, the release of dopamine will reinforce the desire for engagement and connection with the other. One will begin to seek out the relationship and will be eager to connect. When this rewarding connection is deepened through intentional interactions that allow the other to exercise freedom of choice, this is where profound healing and transformation begin to occur, both for the human and the horse.

The crux of Natural Lifemanship's TF-EAP can be summarized as follows:

- We start with the heuristic of the Neurosequential Model to understand the patterns of activation in the brain that are at the root of dysfunction in one's relationship with oneself and with others.

- In the course of building a relationship with the horse, the client begins to learn and to apply the NL principles to create predictability and reward in the relationship. Over repeated interactions, both human and horse form pathways in their brains that tell them that safe, connected and predictable relationships are rewarding and that choosing to act in ways that build the relationship feels good.

- Principles are learned instead of methods or techniques because relationships are unique and dynamic and any given method at any time may be supportive or damaging to a relationship. The principles are always understood in the context of a connected and attuned relationship, as this is the only way one may know the relationship partner intimately enough to discern the being's internal state and to respond appropriately to a given behavior.

In the next part we elaborate on some of the core Natural Lifemanship relationship principles and how they inform the way we partner humans and horses in TF-EAP. Rather than discussing practices, which may or may not resemble techniques employed by other EAP modalities, we focus on the principles beneath practices and the beliefs underlying the principles.

## Part II:

## How the Natural Lifemanship Principles are Used for Creating Connected Relationships that Reorganize the Brains of Both Humans and Horses

As we begin to discuss some of the Natural Lifemanship principles we must emphasize once more that the neurobiology of trauma informs everything we do. The horse's brain is organized in a very similar way to the brain of the client who is in therapy for the purpose of healing trauma. Because relationship and rhythm are needed to heal trauma and to spur new organization in the brain, TF-EAP consists of repeated relational interactions where connection, and thus healing, progress as client and horse learn to be in a relationship with each other in a connected and attuned way. It is a process that takes practice, time, and repetition and requires both parties' presence and full engagement.

The Natural Lifemanship principles provide a problem-solving lens that helps to focus the client's and the therapy team's attention on the relationship dynamics themselves, becoming mindfully aware of how each partner is responding internally to them. Through the process of working to build the relationship guided by these principles, horses and humans enhance each other's capacities for self-regulation and connection within their relationships. Importantly, each of the Natural Lifemanship principles is equally relevant to the relationship whether on the ground or on the back of the horse.

*Because the relationship is the vehicle for change, the relationship between the client and horse must be a real relationship, and real connection is always the goal.*

The relationship with the horse is always a real relationship, never a metaphorical one. Healthy relationships require subject-to-subject authenticity. Each of us desires to be known and loved in truth, not in imagination. Relationships at their superficial level often begin as subject-object where we (subject) form a construct or idea (object) of another being based on first impressions, preconceptions, or stereotypes. As the relationship deepens, our knowledge of the other becomes highly personal; something that is felt and not easily described. A wise teacher once said the more you know and love someone the more it breaks your heart to try to describe her or him. Words become painfully inadequate. There is a difference between *knowing something* and *knowing someone*.

Metaphor is a powerful cognitive and linguistic capacity humans possess allowing us to make sense of and communicate (often quite poetically) complex concepts. It is an exercise in objectification – *a way of knowing something*. It can be a great learning and teaching tool when used appropriately, even in therapy. However, we strongly believe that objectifying another being or any relationship between beings ultimately interferes with true connection and intimacy. Connection is so critical to healing trauma that it needs to be truly present. When we think of the relationship or the other with whom we share the relationship metaphorically, then the actual *sense* of connection (subject-subject knowing) becomes obscured by the *thoughts about* connection (subject-object knowing). In TF-EAP our aim is always to foster true connection.

*Natural Lifemanship defines a good relationship as one that is attuned, connected and co-operative, not compliant.*

The difference between cooperation and compliance is an important distinction in NL. According to Dr. Perry and colleagues (1995), compliance is a dissociative response of the midbrain. As such it cannot be considered a response of the neocortex. Cooperation, on the other hand, is something one chooses and to choose to cooperate with someone requires both neocortical and limbic engagement. Cooperation is both thoughtful and relational. Although compliance may look like cooperation in that both may result in the horse or human performing the behavior that was requested, the difference lies in the part of the brain which is responsible for initiating the desired behavior. Cooperation builds connection, and compliance eventually damages it.

A healthy relationship is an attuned and connected relationship in which each partner chooses cooperation and connection; this is not the same thing as an obedient relationship in which the choice, so to speak, is predetermined by the relationship dynamic whereby one partner assumes a dominant role and the other a submissive or obedient one. Cooperation and connection – not compliance – are the goals of any relationship, including the relationship between human and horse.

The distinction between cooperation and compliance has some major implications for the way in which humans train and handle horses. One is that we never wish to desensitize the horse, nor do we wish to create a dynamic where compliance and submission are their habitual responses to a human. Desensitization is a product of conditioning the horse's dissociative response. Dissociation in horses and in humans is a powerful adaptive stress response state that protects us when it is impossible to escape from inflicted pain or abuse and when resisting would cause more harm. In horses, as in humans, a state (something meant to be temporary) can become a trait (something more fixed and permanent) (Perry, et al., 1995). To acquire the trait of dissociation through routine desensitization interferes profoundly with connection and learning in both species. A dissociative, checked out human or horse cannot be connected, nor can they learn. Likewise, dissociation may feel safe but it does not indeed keep one safe.

Furthermore, because we are very mindful of this distinction between cooperation and compliance, we are circumspect when interpreting a horse's behavior. For example, licking and chewing can at times signal the horse's submissive response to an increase in pressure, and at other times can signal relaxation that will often accompany the release of pressure. Discerning the horse's behavior is therefore a matter of attunement. One must be attuned both to oneself and to the horse to sense and understand the inner experience of each in order to more accurately interpret the dynamic that is occurring between them.

*If it is not good for both partners, it is not good for either, eventually.*

A relationship where one partner gets all of his or her needs met and the other does not is ultimately detrimental to each. There are two kinds of relationship patterns that are not healthy for humans and horses. One is when the human feels the need to control the horse so much that the horse has no choices in the relationship. The horse's needs for autonomy are not being met. The other kind of unhealthy relationship is when the human makes no requests of the horse but instead seeks to provide (treats, affection, autonomy) for the horse without asking anything in return. A one-sided relationship will eventually damage the connection between horse and human and, as a result, neither party will be able to benefit from the relationship.

Adhering to the principles that connection is always the goal and that the relationship must be good for both partners requires the client to be connected with her self. If a client is dysregulated and disconnected from him or herself with either too high body energy or too low body energy, the horse may not connect with the client; it will not feel safe to connect. Because of these overarching principles, the client must learn what connection feels like, observe when it is present or absent, and make the internal changes necessary to become a safe connection for the horse. This takes work, and this work is a major component of reorganizing the brain and healing trauma.

## 6.  The Principle of Choice: Cooperation is Predicated on Choice.

*Cooperation by definition requires that a choice* be made to cooperate (a choice that takes into consideration the good of the relationship and thus is based on a sense of connection). *Compliance, on the other hand, is a submissive gesture* in response to too much pressure, in the presence of which a horse does not truly have a choice. Compliance is more resignation than cooperation. Compliance is a behavior that is learned like other routines are learned – by habit. One does not need to think in order to comply and once a horse (or human for that matter) has made a habit of submission and compliance, he can comply automatically without ever thinking about the relationship or minding the connection. In fact, in many situations that both horses and humans face, compliance works so well to keep pressure at bay that it becomes habit. While compliant behavior is rarely seen as problematic, it is ultimately damaging. It interferes with cortical engagement and limbic engagement and therefore interferes with learning, thinking and connection.

Although horses, at this point in their evolution, are not yet capable of abstract thinking as humans are, they do have a small, primitive frontal lobe. Their frontal lobe has not evolved as ours has because it is not needed to survive in their natural habitat, where thinking would interfere with the quick, reactive impulses needed to survive in a world of predators. Horses learn by habit and discriminate their surroundings over time. *"Learning proceeds gradually as the horse learns the relevant dimensions of the problem"* (Black & Peters, 2012).

For a horse in a relationship with humans, pressure is the problem; they seek to learn the dimensions of where it exists and how to avoid it. Natural Lifemanship teaches that choice, cooperation and connection may come to be understood by the horse as relevant dimensions of the problem of pressure in relationships with humans. In other words, when given the opportunity horses will gradually learn that exercising choice (e.g., thinking for themselves) and choosing cooperation and connection enable them not only to successfully navigate pressure, but also to experience deep intrinsic reward in the connection. They may have learned from past experiences that humans either expect their compliance, or they expect nothing from them. We seek to teach them that we expect them to choose to do the right thing for the relationship, which is always connection and cooperation, and we teach this through the NL principles.

Humans who have experienced complex trauma are similar to horses. They have developed a habitual reactive nature that has allowed them to survive in unsafe or unpredictable environments, but this has compromised their capacity to think, to learn and to participate in healthy relationships. A connected relationship built on NL principles teaches both client and horse the relevant dimensions of connected and attuned relationships. Like any other region of the brain, the neocortex develops by use and association. As these dimensions are learned and experienced in frequent relational interactions, the neocortex is used and thus develops. We believe that through frequent relational interactions guided by these dimensions, or principles, the horse's neocortex develops in ways that help the horse to become better at solving problems and making choices, including choices that serve the good of the relationship. This is exactly what happens for the human, as well.

*To teach a horse how to connect and cooperate with us, we must always give the horse the ability to respond to a request by exercising any of his available options – the choice to ignore, to resist, or to cooperate.*

As mentioned, cooperation must be a choice. It is also a learned behavior in the sense that if cooperation does not result in rewarding consequences, it will not be an attractive option for the horse or the human. If it is not rewarding, it will not be practiced and it will not be learned. In Natural Lifemanship, *the release of pressure is the reward* and is the only appropriate response on the part of the human when the horse cooperates. Experienced consistently, this teaches the horse that cooperation is rewarding. The principle of pressure constrained by the principle of choice dictates that *the least amount of pressure is always used to initiate a request*. If a request is made with too much pressure, the horse has no option to ignore it. In this case the horse will either resist or comply, both lower brain reactions. By starting out with the smallest amount of pressure (pressure the horse can easily ignore), the human increases it gradually until the horse chooses not to ignore, at which time the choice is rewarded with a release of pressure.

Not ignoring, or engagement, is just the beginning of relationship. To build the relationship it is natural over time to ask for more trust and more sustained connection. We may first ask the horse to notice us, and then to attach – to be near us or to follow us – to initiate the relationship. Relationships are progressively intimate, however. A deeper level of connection is possible when we ask for detachment (i.e., when we move away from the horse or when we ask the horse to move away from us). Because we care most about the connection, and not the task, we must ourselves be attuned to whether the horse is responding to our requests with connection and cooperation, or by ignoring us, or with resistance or compliance. Only when the horse cooperates with connection is it appropriate for us to release the pressure.

There are some principles of behavior modification at play in this process. For example, by making the reward the release of pressure, we are employing a type of negative reinforcement. However, we depart from traditional behavior modification in many ways. For one, the goal is not modifying a behavior; the goal is connection, which we facilitate by reinforcing a new pattern of behavior in the brain. We aim to help the brain associate the rewarding release of pressure with the choice to connect and freely cooperate with a request. The request itself is made for the purpose of building a connected relationship. The goal, for example, is not for the horse to follow me or to move away from me, or to perform any task for me. The goal is to build a more attuned and trusting relationship in which the horse is willing to follow me or move away from me when I ask, just as I am willing to respond to her requests when she asks.

*On whether or not the horse truly has a choice if the only way to get pressure released is through cooperation...*

This question understandably arises. However, we believe a connected relationship is fundamentally good. It is good for the human, and it is good for the horse. When those we love carry relational scars that make it hard for them to enjoy a healthy connection, it is neither caring nor connecting to leave this condition unchallenged.

Take for example our own children. In hurt, anger or frustration they may demand we leave them alone or let them run away. We understand the strong emotions and reactive patterns that drive these impulses, but to honor them would be to allow our loved ones to disconnect, which is ultimately damaging to the relationship we share. Space can be granted if that is what is needed, but it must be granted in a connected way. Allowing our children or horses or clients or others to disconnect whenever their survival instincts demand it ultimately reinforces the wrong pathways in the brain. It essentially teaches them that they can escape from the pressure within the relationship by disconnecting from the relationship. When these pathways are reinforced, they set up a pattern that affects how the individual or horse responds to stress in all relationships, not just our relationship.

It is for this reason that we are not opposed to using enclosed spaces such as round pens for sessions when building a relationship with a horse. Round pens aren't to contain the horse as much as they are to enable the person to communicate the principles of pressure appropriately while building the relationship. At a certain stage in the relationship or in the person's ability to manage his or her body energy skillfully, a round pen may not be needed or even what is best for the relationship.

In TF-EAP, client-horse relationships may start in the open pasture and progress to the round pen, and then move to the open pasture again. They may start on the ground and move to the back of the horse. Or, they may start on the back of the horse, move to the ground, and return to mounted. They may never leave the ground. Each relationship presents different dynamics and reveals different needs. The therapy team must be highly attuned to these dynamics and flexible in using the NL principles together with specific therapy modalities to guide treatment.

## 7.   How a Horse May Experience the NL Principles on the Ground

In TF-EAP, when relational work with the horse is guided by NL principles, both client and horse will learn to navigate certain dimensions within relationships. Some of these dimensions from the horse's perspective (albeit anthropomorphized) may be as follows:

- Relationships with humans naturally come with some pressure (an expectation to relate or to interact brings some amount of pressure).

- When I feel pressure, I always have a choice in how to respond.

- I can try different answers to figure out how to get the pressure released. I can trust that so long as I'm trying, the pressure won't increase. I am safe to explore options.

- Ignoring the pressure does not work. The pressure increases if I ignore it.

- Submission and compliance do not work. The pressure stays the same. I have to keep searching.

- Running away from a human who wants to have a relationship with me does not work. Because they care about our relationship, they may create a smaller boundary so I can make better choices.

- Connection feels good. When I start to connect, some of the pressure gets released. When I stay connected, I can try to resist in many different ways, but the pressure will stay the same. Connection feels safe and predictable.

- Cooperation with connection feels really, really good. The pressure completely goes away. Dopamine and oxytocin flood my body. All that searching for the right answer was worth it. I will soon become eager to cooperate and to connect with my human. I may even start to become curious about connecting differently with members of my herd.

## 8.   How the Principles Extend to Mounted Work

### How and Why we use Mounted Work

We typically use groundwork to allow the client and horse to practice connection and to build a relationship. However, there are times that the client is ready to explore a deeper connection with the horse through mounted work. There are other times we use mounted work for the purpose of regulating a client who is unable to connect with the horse, even on the ground. In these cases we help the client begin to connect with herself and develop the capacity for self-regulation. We are very mindful, however, that the horse needs a safe connection. In TF-EAP mounted sessions, the EP must be able to maintain the connection with a horse who has a highly dysregulated (e.g., anxious or dissociative) client on her back. The EP must be able to fluidly take over connection and transfer it back to the client as the client becomes able to safely connect. This requires skill and that the EP maintain attunement with the horse and with the client. In TF-EAP, cultivating attuned connection is essential for everyone involved in the process.

Rhythm and connected relationships are needed to activate the lower regions of the brain, reorganize the stress response system and heal trauma. Through connection, especially during mounted work, clients may begin to co-regulate with the horse, much in the same way infants and young children co-regulate with their primary caregivers. The implication for treating the relationship with the horse as a real relationship is that the horse is never used as a means to an end. Both the ends and means of TF-EAP is the building of a connected, attuned relationship; the physiological benefits accrue in the process.

Every Natural Lifemanship principle that applies when a client and horse interact on the ground is equally relevant during mounted work. While the trend in the equine world seems to be toward increasingly relational approaches to working with horses on the ground, it remains deeply challenging for most humans to not feel the need to control the horse as soon as we are sitting on his or her back. It is quite natural because we are indeed the most vulnerable while on the horse's back. From a relational perspective, mounted is where we may experience the deepest connection and also the most fear. Being mounted introduces a mild amount of stress, known as eustress. This makes it possible for the client to practice self regulation skills under eustress while benefiting from the passive regulation provided by the horse's rhythmic, repetitive, patterned gait. The connection while on the horse's back evokes physical closeness, vulnerability and trust. Furthermore, it facilitates sensory integration and trauma processing in powerful ways. Because mounted work is at the same time so potentially therapeutic and yet so challenging when it comes to applying NL principles, we offer some of the specific ways we facilitate for the client the transfer of principles from the ground to the times when they are mounted.

First, as we mentioned earlier, the role of the EP becomes especially critical during mounted work. The EP must be able to give and to take connection with the horse and to sense when either is appropriate. Even more importantly, the EP must be able to lead the horse while on the ground and while mounted without feeling the need to rely on power, domination, or control.

For the client who is mounted, experiencing attunement and connection with the horse while riding may be as close as he or she can come to benefiting from critical experiences that may have been missing in infancy – that of being held, rocked and soothed by a nurturing caregiver who is attuned to the infant's needs. Mounted work with connection may, therefore, be a powerful form of re-parenting for some, therapeutically speaking. When clients have difficulty with connection while mounted, we may scaffold or help their sense of connection in a number of ways. One way is that we very often start by asking the client to drape her body over the back of the horse (arms and head on one side and legs on the other) to begin to experience the sensation of connection and safety while allowing the horse to support one's body. Next, we may have the client sit on the horse bareback, or with a bareback pad. This allows them to be in closer contact with the horse and also removes the saddle, which may give the illusion of control. We also have the EP on the other end of a lead rope, which greatly lessens for the client the sense of needing to control the horse. They are willing to relinquish control and instead trust in the connection between the horse and the EP, and eventually between themselves and the horse. Sometimes before we practice any self regulation skills, and often when ending a mounted session, we give the client time to face backward and drape their body over the horse's rump. This can be deeply relaxing and very connecting for both the client and the horse.

For the horse, staying connected with the rider in this way creates and reinforces patterns that allow the horse to remain connected while detached. Similarly, it allows people the opportunity to practice connection even while feeling vulnerable and dysregulated. Each eventually learns that there can be safety in connection, even when the relationship is at its most intimate and vulnerable.

When connection ceases to be the primary focus and the horse is simply being used as if she were a rhythm producing machine, or a rocking chair, then the horse is learning that relationships with a being sitting on its back do not feel rewarding and may even feel unsafe. At the same time, on a psychological level, the human is learning that connection is unimportant and that relationships exist only to help meet personal needs. On a physiological level, the effort required to maintain a conscious intention to connect is what activates the limbic regions of the brains of both parties in the relationship. The limbic area when activated facilitates integration and cross-brain connections for both partners.

## 9. Summary

The principles that inform the horse-human interactions in Natural Lifemanship's TF-EAP derive equally from two heuristics: trauma-informed neuroscience (in particular the Neurosequential Model of Development) and the NL principles for building healthy, connected relationships. The beneficial effects of building and of experiencing a connected relationship can do no other than accrue to both parties of the relationship. Humans who have experienced complex trauma and horses are especially ideal relationship partners. They each enter the relationship with similar neurological patterns conditioned by having learned and/or having evolved to survive in a world of threat and danger. Natural Lifemanship principles help the human and horse learn to build a relationship characterized by connection, not by survival instincts. The process of doing so results in profound healing, growth and development for each.

**About the Authors**

Tim Jobe, BS – A pioneer in the field of Equine Assisted Psychotherapy, Tim has worked training horses for over 40 years and has helped youth and families overcome adverse life circumstances through EAP for over 25 years. He is one of the founding board members of the Equine Assisted Growth and Learning Association (EAGALA). He co-developed Natural Lifemanship based on his experiences working with youth and horses, through which he came to understand that the way in which the client builds the relationship with the horse profoundly impacts the therapeutic outcomes accruing from the relationship. Natural Lifemanship horse training principles are specifically designed to apply equally to horse and human relationships, resulting in deeply therapeutic work in the mental health field. Tim spends most of his time teaching the Natural Lifemanship model to others and mentoring EPs and therapists who are practicing and becoming certified in TF-EAP. Tim and his wife Bettina are actively growing the Natural Lifemanship organization to meet the increasing demand as word about this model's effectiveness spreads.

Bettina is a licensed and certified mental health counselor with extensive training and experience using therapies known to be effective in the treatment of trauma. She has effectively incorporated Equine Assisted Psychotherapy for over 10 years to treat clients with significant trauma histories. As co-founder of Natural Lifemanship and the author of a seminal research study on EAP, she is committed to including horses in the therapy process in ways that are evidence-based and backed by sound research. This has contributed to a model in which every aspect of the horse, including its psychology and its physiology, is employed very intentionally to help clients heal from the psychological and the physiological insults of trauma. Bettina extensively trains and supervises therapists and therapy teams that are using Natural Lifemanship and/or who are seeking certification in TF-EAP. Together with Tim Jobe she is also supporting a growing cadre of certified Natural Lifemanship trainers. Tim and Bettina have co-authored multiple books and papers and are widely sought after speakers and trainers in the world of trauma treatment and EAP. They live in Liberty Hill, Texas where they raise dogs, chickens, horses and a toddler.

Laura McFarland, PhD – Laura's passion and expertise are related to the effective education of adults through transformative learning. Transformative learning is education that impacts not only what we know, but also our understandings of self, of others, and of the belief systems that influence our ways of seeing and being in our personal and professional lives. Transformative learning almost always involves what is understood as a paradigm shift.

Since attending her first NL training in 2010, Laura has been committed to understanding and promoting the paradigm shift that is frequently attributed to Natural Lifemanship by those who undergo training and certification in the model. She is equally committed to furthering the research and evaluation needed to assess the impact of TF-EAP treatment on mental health outcomes and to establish its evidence base. Since childhood, Laura has found deep meaning in her connection with horses and with all of nature. She is profoundly grateful to be in a position to advance a mental health therapy model and a transformative learning approach that are centered on the connection between humans and horses.

Laura completed her doctorate in Multicultural Special Education at The University of Texas at Austin. Much of her work there focused on culturally responsive pedagogy, including the role of critical self-reflection and experiential learning in the preparation of teachers to serve culturally and linguistically diverse youth with and without disabilities.

## References

Black, Martin and Peters, Stephen. (2012). *Evidence-based horsemanship*. Wasteland Press: Shelbyville, KY.

Perry, B. D. (2001). The neuroarcheology of childhood maltreatment: The neuro-developmental costs of adverse childhood events. In K. Franey, R. Geffner, & R. Falconer (Eds.), *The cost of maltreatment: Who pays? We all do* (pp. 1537). San Diego, CA: Family Violence and Sexual Assault Institute.

Perry, B. D. (2002). Childhood experience and the expression of genetic potential: What childhood neglect tells us about nature and nurture. *Brain and Mind, 3*, 79-100.

Perry, B. D. (2006). The neurosequential model of therapeutics: Applying principles of neuroscience to clinical work with traumatized and maltreated children. In N. Boyd-Webb (Ed.), *Working with traumatized youth in child welfare* (pp. 2752). New York: Guilford Press.

Perry, B. D. (2008). Child maltreatment: The role of abuse and neglect in developmental psychopathology. In T. P. Beauchaine & S. P. Hinshaw (Eds.), *Textbook of child and adolescent psychopathology* (pp. 93128). New York: Wiley.

Perry, Bruce D. (2009). Examining Child Maltreatment Through a Neurodevelopmental Lens: Clinical Applications of the Neurosequential Model of Therapeutics. *Journal of Loss and Trauma, 14*(4), 240255. doi:10.1080/15325020903004350

Perry, B. D., Pollard, R. A., Blakley, T. L., Baker, W. L., & Vigilante, D. (1995). Childhood trauma, the neurobiology of adaptation, and "use-dependent" development of the brain: How "states" become "traits". *Infant mental health journal, 16*(4), 271-291.

# CONCLUSION

At the end of this year's (2017) three-day symposium, participants left with more questions than answers. However, they also came away with more information, new ideas, expanded awareness and perceptions, leads for different approaches they may be interested in pursuing further training in, and a deeper and more nuanced appreciation for equines, their needs, and the depth of their contributions in therapy and learning programs. 28 contributions – by practitioners in our field. Various backgrounds, various practices, various points of view. No preference, no order, no corrections. Just like the horses deserve to have a voice that may be contradictory to other people's viewpoints, it is important to lend an ear to all viewpoints, without censoring, correcting or editing. Just like at this year's and future symposiums, the reader may not have gotten one answer – but the opportunity to walk away from this book with enough knowledge to form a unique individual opinion, like and dislike.